HAIR TRAFFIC CONTROL

HAIR TRAFFIC CONTROL

A MEMOIR

LIZZI MAC

Copyright © 2024 by Lizzi Mac

ALL RIGHTS RESERVED. This book contains material protected under international and federal copyright laws. Any unauthorised reprint or use of this material is prohibited. No part of this book may be reproduced or transmitted in any form or by any means, electronic or mechanical, including photocopying, recording, or by an information and retrieval system without express written permission from the Author, except for the use of brief quotations in a book review. This is a work of fiction. Names, characters, places, and incidents are the product of the author's imagination or are used fictitiously, and any resemblance to actual persons, living or dead, business establishments, events, or locales is entirely coincidental.

Cover design and illustration: Emma Andrews

Copywriter: Gideon D'arfft

Dev & line edits/Interior formatting: Ivy Graves

Beta readers: Angela Booth, Yvi Dee, Jane Mc Dermid

This book is for my family,

who made me, shaped me,

and continue to make me proud.

CONTENTS

Author's Note — xiii

1. COME FLY WITH ME — 1
   FRANK SINATRA
2. I HAVE A DREAM — 17
   ABBA
3. DOWN UNDER — 23
   MEN AT WORK
4. ON ILKLEY MOOR BAHT' 'AT — 37
   SILKSTONE BRASS BAND
5. LIFE IN A NORTHERN TOWN — 53
   DREAM ACADEMY
6. DEVIL'S HAIRCUT — 61
   BECK
7. IT MUST HAVE BEEN LOVE — 67
   ROXETTE
8. FASHION — 83
   DAVID BOWIE
9. LIVE AID — 97
   DO THEY KNOW IT'S CHRISTMAS
10. 9 TO 5 — 107
    DOLLY PARTON
11. BUFFALO STANCE — 117
    NENEH CHERRY
12. SHE WORKS HARD FOR THE MONEY — 129
    DONNA SUMMER

13. CALLING OCCUPANTS OF INTERPLANETARY CRAFT
THE CARPENTERS — 137

14. THUNDERSTRUCK
AC/DC — 151

15. CAKE BY THE OCEAN
DNCE — 157

16. PUMP IT UP
ELVIS COSTELLO & THE ATTRACTIONS — 167

17. HERE I GO AGAIN
WHITESNAKE — 175

18. MAGICAL MYSTERY TOUR
THE BEATLES — 187

19. WE DON'T HAVE TO TAKE OUR CLOTHES OFF
JERMAINE STEWART — 197

20. SHOULD I STAY OR SHOULD I GO
THE CLASH — 207

21. BIG LOVE
FLEETWOOD MAC — 215

22. THE VOICE WITHIN
CHRISTINA AGUILERA — 221

23. MAMBO NO.5 (A LITTLE BIT OF...)
LOU BEGA — 229

24. BABOOSHKA
KATE BUSH — 235

25. BEAUTIFUL LIAR
BEYONCE, SHAKIRA — 245

26. TITANIUM
SIA | DAVID GUETTA — 257

27. CRY ME OUT   269
    PIXI LOTT
28. GOLD DUST WOMAN   279
    STEVIE NICKS
29. LONG AND WINDING ROAD   289
    THE BEATLES
30. DON'T YOU FORGET
    ABOUT ME   299
    SIMPLE MINDS
31. GYPSY   313
    STEVIE NICKS
32. THAT'S WHAT FRIEND'S
    ARE FOR   321
    DIONNE WARWICK
33. HERO   327
    MARIAH CAREY

Acknowledgments   333
Dear Reader   335

AUTHOR'S NOTE

Dear Reader,

This year marks my 40th year in hairdressing. A milestone that comes with plenty of stories and, thankfully, just enough credibility to convince you I know what I'm talking about. A year ago, I realised I'd amassed enough material to fill a book (or at least a decent magazine), so here we are.

I wanted to give you a front-row seat to the dazzling and vibrant world of hairdressing. It's a place of triumphs, mishaps, and moments that have made me laugh, cry, or just sit in a dark room with a stiff drink. But this book isn't just about foils and fades, and the perfect blowout.

Life has a habit of barging into the salon, uninvited, so you'll also find a few personal tales sprinkled throughout – those messy, hilarious collisions between family, career, and life itself. Because let's face it: Instagram and TikTok may sell you a glossy, filter-perfect version of life, but for the rest of us? We're muddling through, trying not to trip over the hair dryer cord.

My love of storytelling goes way back to my school days. Sport and English were my favourite subjects. One let me run wild, the other gave me the words to explain why I'd done it.

I had a cracking English teacher, Mr Nightingale, who was stingy with giving top marks but brilliant at making you work for them. Thanks to him, I fell in love with words and even Shakespeare; I get it! But what I truly adore is a good story. Real, raw, and funny, preferably told around a campfire, though I'll settle for a salon chair. And trust me, this job has delivered them by the bucket load.

To you brave souls who just bought this book – thank you. I hope you enjoy it, especially my fellow hairdressers. I'm still here in the trenches with you, dodging disasters, riding the storm, and laughing through it all. Feel free to grab a cup of tea, a glass of wine, or something stronger if your day calls for it (no judgment). This is life behind the chair, warts and all, with a healthy dose of gritty humour and zero pretence.

Welcome to Hair Traffic Control. Follow the QR code for more fun.

LM

Instagram for some fun extras

Spotify Playlist to set the mood

1

COME FLY WITH ME

FRANK SINATRA

WELCOME aboard everyone on flight 10/81. Buckle up, because you are about to embark on a journey that has nothing to do with tropical beaches or European cities. No, today's destination is far more elusive and infinitely more challenging. The land of the perfect blonde. Please ensure your seats are in the upright position, tray tables stowed, and seat belts firmly fastened.

Wella's Colour Touch 10/81 and 10/6. They're not just names; they're my secret weapons, my 'Go to' my 'save the day'!

They whisk me away to a realm of hair colouring magic, ensuring I get the perfect result every time. Like a trusty co-pilot, these tubes of hair craft essentials are a must in any stylist's treasure chest.

They're like the equivalent of first-class seats with unlimited champagne.

But before we break out the bubbly and delve into the world of toners, we must conquer the bleaching process and achieve that clean, even lift. This is no mere layover; it's the crucial first leg of the journey.

Picture it: the bleach is applied, the foils are in place; the clock is ticking. It's a delicate dance, part science, part alchemy, and 100% nerve-wracking.

A clean lift sets the stage for what's coming, and trust me if you don't nail it, you might as well kiss that dream of a buttery blonde goodbye.

Now once you've landed that bleach job without incident, it's time for the toners to take centre aisle.

And let me tell you, they are the divas of this operation – temperamental, high-maintenance, and prone to stealing the show. They move with visual precision, and you, the navigator, must be confident in your choice. Not too flat, not too ash, with a nice gloss finish. The toner is a destination, so it's important we are on the correct flight path.

These toners are my ground control. They perform with precision, painting a symphony of shades that complement the landscape beneath.

The landscape is the base colour – It's important to understand your terrain and how far you can push the base shade in either direction without compromising the hair condition.

And let's not forget, the skies of hair colour are crowded, and every brand is up there, flying at you like discount airline offers. Each one boasts a vast selection, offering every shade of the rainbow, and as diverse as the clients that sit in your chair. I've flirted with them all from the classics to the new kids on the block, and let me tell you, nothing will turn your smile upside down faster than a toner gone rogue - over-depositing, leaving the once vibrant highlight flat or tinted with an unwelcome purple.

A misstep can mean disaster, but a well-chosen toner. It's the difference between "Meh," and "Wow!"

In our world, we speak a cryptic language of numbers and "letters" as we navigate the colour wheel with finesse. It's a lexicon shared among hairdressers separating the pros from the wannabes – a well-worn flight manual and secret code that guides us to the perfect shade for each desired outcome, and a smooth landing.

My journey in hairdressing took off in the vibrant, dynamic, and exciting 1980s, and I can assure you that this was no ordinary decade. It was a neon-soaked era where big hair ruled and shoulder pads made everyone look like an NFL linebacker. Amidst this glamorous chaos, the salon I called home embraced Wella as its flagship brand.

> This is where I first laid eyes on my new bible, the Wella shade chart.

Those little numbers and letters became the notes in the melody of my early career, and to this day, that language remains etched in the core of my craft.

Now, if you've never stood behind a salon chair, I cordially invite you to step into our world for a glimpse of our colour wall – a hairdresser's heaven. To the untrained eye, it's just a neat row of pretty tubes. We see them as highly pigmented concoctions, just begging to be squeezed and mixed into something magical. We stand there, pupils dilated, hands twitching like we are about to paint the Sistine Chapel. These pigments aren't just colours – they're promises. Promises that your hair will come out looking exactly like the vision we had for you since you walked through the door.

Whether you wanted to look like Madonna or the girl next door (or, let's be honest, sometimes both) Wella had our backs.

Now, let's be clear: when I say "vision", I don't mean some generic "Oh, let's just brighten her up a bit." No, darling. I'm talking about a full-blown, Hollywood-worthy, red-carpet-ready transformation that syncs perfectly with your personality, lifestyle, and – let's not forget – budget. It's like matchmaking but with hair dye.

Of course, there's a bit of hair colouring sorcery involved, too. This is alchemy, after all! The first rule of colour club: what you see in the bowl is not what you will see on your result. It's the ultimate optical illusion. Coppers? They can start as a murky purple. And black? That often begins as a shocking yellow.

> Naturally, this can cause wide-eyed panic from the person in the chair, blindly trusting us with their hair destiny.

So, I take them on the scenic tour of the process, pointing out the sights like a seasoned tour guide.

"Yes, it's purple now, but trust me, it's on its way to being a rich copper red. You might want to rethink your wardrobe, though. This hue may need more pizzazz than just black, black, and more black."

And after all that fantastic advice about branching out beyond black, here we hairdressers stand - draped head to toe in, you guessed it, black. But there's a method to our monochrome madness. You see, black is our best friend. Got a bleach stain on your uniform? No problem. Just toss it in the washer with some black dye, and voila - good as new. Or if you're pressed for time (and who isn't) a quick scribble with a sharpie will hide the evidence. Any other colour though, and we're done for. White? Forget it. One stray drop of dye, and you're basically wearing a tie-dye tribute to chaos. Catch it early, douse it in hairspray to zap the offending stain, and there's a chance it may just wash out.

Now, we have fancy colour wipes, those little miracle workers that erase stain residue from the client's hairline. But back in the day, we weren't so high-tech. Oh no, we were resourceful, fabulous even.

When a client's hairline was looking more like a crime scene, we would simply dip a wet corner of a towel straight into the nearest ashtray (an ancient salon ritual) and lovingly massage it in, something about carbon science, and recycling of course. Was it glamorous? Not exactly. Hygienic? Let's not dwell on that. Just a gritty elegant hack in a time when salons had ashtrays, and it effectively got the job done.

But here's the thing about Wella: Their Koleston Perfect colour range stands as a beacon in the salon world. Even as other brands try to mimic its glorious colour spectrum, Koleston Perfect remains an industry leader, proudly showcased in the aisle of hairdressing suppliers everywhere.

And let's not forget, as consumer awareness grows – thank you, social media, everyone's become a hair scientist, scrutinising ingredients like they're about to start their own lab. Clients come in armed with more knowledge than a contestant on a game show, tossing out terms like "ammonia-free, organic, and vegan," faster than I can mix their toner. It's enough to make your head spin faster than a salon chair.

The Wella colour chart has had quite a glow-up since I first started. Back in the day, the hottest ticket in town was Titian red. Let me tell you, I was always sneakily eyeing the appointment book, plotting who I could subtly convert to this daring hue.

> You've had a coffee? Great, let's make you a redhead.

The shade chart has evolved since then. With the passage of time, the Titian red formula as I knew it has gone the way of perms and shoulder pads. Now, it's all posh colours with twice the vibrancy and reflect, and names that sound like cocktails at a rooftop bar. Even the toners have upped their game. Back in the day, we toned with semi and demi-permanents.

Nowadays, it's gone all science-y, you can even skip the brush and bottle application and pop a toning pod into the shower head, turning your rinse into a high-tech colourful spa experience. Very snazzy, and frankly, a bit show-offy. And why not!

But back in the day, for some reason, we preferred colour shades with warmth, to compliment the client's skin tone. If it came out too ashy, that was basically a national emergency. We'd gather around the chair like surgeons, whispering, "Is that grey?" like it was the worst thing imaginable.

Fast forward to today, and people stride in asking for Fifty Shades of Granny Grey. I mean, who could have predicted that?

We stylists are a resilient bunch, though, always up for a challenge – unless, of course, you've been worshipping at the altar of the dark brown box dye and now want to go lighter. That, my friends, is no longer a challenge. It's straight-up missionary work!

BUT BEING a hairdresser is not for those of weak spirit. The salon is a fast-paced, high-stakes environment, leaving one constantly on edge. It's like when you're waiting impatiently at baggage claim for your suitcase, eyes darting and your head swirling with the possibility of a stranger nicking your case and waltzing off with your favourite pair of shoes.

Now swap that scene, multiply it by ten, and you've got A Day in the Life of a Stylist. It's a constant hustle to make sure everyone's suitcase – I mean, hair – arrives on time and in perfect condition.

The salon is like a busy airport in some ways, complete with its own version of TSA (Totally Sassy Attitudes). Every day, clients arrive for check-in. Our regulars, the ones that could navigate the salon with their eyes closed. They're our frequent flyers, breezing in for their weekly blow dry, and a chin-wag. They're in and out faster than you can say "volumizing mousse". Then there are the six-weekers, the ones who show up like clockwork for a trim, a colour refresher, and maybe a few foils if they're feeling fancy. They are our bread and butter, the dependable ones, like those flights that always board on time and land without a hitch.

> But then enter the wild cards – the client who pops in every few months, just to remind us they still exist.

These are the restyles, the ones who want to go from brunette to blonde or chop off six inches on a whim. They're like international flights that suddenly appear on your itinerary; exciting, but you know there's potential for some turbulence.

Our clients are just like flights, as one plane leaves, another one hits the tarmac. We're the pilot, the flight attendants, and ground crew, all rolled into one. Hustling to keep everyone moving smoothly, ensuring no one is stuck on the runway longer than necessary. And while we're at it, let's talk about punctuality. We love a client who arrives at our "Hair Port" gate, fresh faced and ready for take-off. But we get it – life happens, and sometimes that skinny latte can't be ignored.

All we ask is that you factor in those precious ten minutes, because once you're late, the whole salon schedule starts to look like a delayed flight board at Heathrow.

Once aboard the 'Hair Plane', we hope that through our consultation, we can take you to your dream destination. We're your friendly travel agents, minus the dodgy brochures. We just hope our flight doesn't get hijacked before take off by Instagram filtered fantasy pics that have no place on any flight.

Let me tell you, nothing sends a hairdresser into a cold sweat faster than a client with a Pinterest board full of fantasies and a vocabulary limited to "just like this, but better."

Like passengers, our clients have places to go after their appointment. Whether it's back to the grindstone, a night out with the girls, a special event, or even a dream holiday on their bucket list. Bottom line, they're on a journey and we are here to make sure it's an enjoyable one.

We offer our own version of in-flight entertainment, a natter about anything and everything, along with refreshments, and the luxury of extra legroom. And don't forget, we provide free Wi-Fi, because what's a good salon visit without the thrill of pretending you're at work? We fully support the art of sneaking in some "productivity" while you're on mute, tapping away with one earphone in. And if you need to go live on zoom, we'll duck out of the frame quick-fast.

We've shared countless journeys together with our clients – some bold enough to rival a mid-life crisis, from daring hair experiments to regular touch-ups, and we are always here to keep things on course. We've weathered the stormy skies of Births, Deaths, and Marriages – and the occasional I'm-single-and-loving-it divorce.

In fact, we've become so well versed in your life stories, we could diagnose most health issues on the fly. Consider it a mini-medical consultation before we finally admit that google isn't a licensed physician.

And much like flights, sometimes appointments get delayed, cancelled or rescheduled. It happens. But we do soften the blow with surprise perks – like a last-minute VIP conditioning treatment, complete with a head massage so blissful it might make you forget why you needed to see a real doctor in the first place.

And let's be honest, it buys us a bit of time if we are running fashionably late.

But believe me, not every stylist is salon-ready right out of the gate. It takes time, patience, and a few awkwardly short bangs along the way to get there. Some might get a bit scissor-happy, miss the brief, and suddenly you've got a fringe that belongs in a witness protection program.

After forty years in the hairdressing game, I've encountered a parade of delightful and eccentric clients that keep me tethered to this industry.

> The deal is: it all starts with a good solid haircut.

Most people have a clear picture of what they want, and they even appreciate a healthy dose of honesty. Bringing a reference picture and chatting over a colour chart? Now that's a winning strategy. The language of hairdressing has evolved. I don't see the point in dazzling clients with elaborate descriptions of techniques or blinding them with science. They're not here for a TED talk – they just want to be the best version of themselves without having to re-mortgage their house.

But let's get real, not every client and hairdresser are on the same page, or even reading the same book, for that matter. Occasionally, we encounter a difficult client who's more trouble than a wasp at a picnic. The no-shows or constant changing appointments last minute, leaving gaps in our day (and our bank accounts)

We aim for realistic results, but when the client has their headset on the stars with a budget that barely covers the launch pad, we quickly yank their head out of the clouds.

We're a business, after all, with overheads and many years of training behind us, not a magical wand shop. And let's be honest, flashing photos at me of your hair twenty years ago – back when you were single, carefree, and blissfully unaware of marriage, kids, and life's eventual sucker punch, isn't exactly a fair fight.

And finally, we come to that client - the bane of every stylist's existence.

> You know the one. The head-wobbler.

The human bobblehead who gives you motion sickness while you are trying to foil their hair.

Their hand-talking, giggling, and suddenly lurching forward to rummage in their bag - right when you're working on the top foils.

And heaven forbid they face the mirror like a normal person.

No. They're craning their neck around to lock eyes with you, like some kind of needy owl.

Meanwhile, we are silently screaming:

> Sit Freakin' Still!!

Because trust us- we do not have time to fix the disaster you're about to cause.

By this point, every stylist's blood pressure has shot through the roof, and we're considering whether 'head brace installation' could be offered as an add-on service.

In those rare cases, we don't hesitate to power up the salon rocket and send these space cadets on a one-way trip to the outer stratosphere – After all, some clients, like passengers, are better off in orbit.

So, why did I embark on the path of hairdressing?

Buckle up people, and of course, my fellow hair crew around the globe, as we prepare for take-off.

I invite you to sit back, relax and enjoy the flight. We'll be cruising at an altitude of perfect blonde, with a strong tailwind of experience and a clear path ahead, or so we tell ourselves.

Now, I can't promise we'll reach our destination without a hitch, but I can guarantee some laughs and a few insights along the way.

Just remember to be kind to our trolley dollies – oops, I mean stylists. They're the ones keeping this ship in the sky, armed with only a comb, some foils, and a prayer. And who knows? By the end of this flight, we might just land somewhere fabulous.

Wheels up, and off we go!

I will be back shortly with a refreshment of your choice, and a selection of magazines. Enjoy your trip!

2

I HAVE A DREAM

ABBA

ALTHOUGH I WAS BORN in Brisbane, Australia, my early roots trace back to England - the small town of Barnsley, South Yorkshire, where I was the youngest of four sisters.

My passion for hair ignited at the tender age of seven, running errands for a lady named Renee Timms, a retired hairdresser and a neighbour who lived a few doors away.

Renee, battling a lung disease, relied on my supermarket runs. She handpicked me for her missions, which often included a cheeky purchase of cigarettes in the carefree 1970s – an era which had no qualms about sending a young lass on such ventures, as long as I had a shopping list to show to the shopkeeper. My reward for this was a coin or two, along with forging a unique bond with Renee – a connection so genuine that it earned my mother's approval to keep her company. She had a son who visited fortnightly, and I became her honorary relative in his absence.

As the daughter of a nurse who worked night shifts and a father who worked away, Renee's house became my haven. She taught me the art of playing cards. Games like, Rummy and Blackjack, all for the prize of old copper two pence pieces, as we sipped tea while indulging in biscuits.

Staying over meant sleeping on a luxurious feather sofa, feeling like a modern-day princess. The Emerald green fabric, threaded with a ridiculously regal gold embossed pattern, was cool to touch – the sort of cool that whispers, " Don't even think about eating any snacks on me." The plush cushions were big and bouncy – the perfect pillow for an amateur queen. Nothing before, or ever since, has come close to that level of unrestrained luxury.

Renee was kind-hearted. She took me under her wing and treated me like one of her own. Her independence and savvy attitude intrigued me. She would whip up appetising, mouth-watering meals whilst I did a few chores. This involved trips to the outdoor bunker to keep the coal bucket topped up, tending the fire, and sweeping the coal dust from the hearth with her very posh brass companion set. Considering the historical feat of some poor unfortunate children being sent up the chimneys to sweep them, this was, easy street.

I had the esteemed job of pushing around her Eubank carpet sweeper, a marvel of engineering free of electricity or batteries – a handy tool that, like disco music, disappeared in the '80s.

She had a knack for cutting through the nonsense, dishing out life's lessons like she was serving up biscuits – simple, satisfying, and just what I needed. She made me feel as if I could conquer anything I set my mind to, from life's goals to mastering her shopping lists. Whether it was handling her post office business, collecting her pension to paying her bills, she made it feel like a grand adventure that came with great responsibility. The generational gap? Well, it vanished the moment she smiled, like a warm, wise grandma you never knew you needed, complete with all the charm and wisdom one could hope for.

In her home, tucked away at the rear, we shared moments that were cosy and inspirational. Every so often, Renee would plonk me on a stool, and give my hair a tidy-up, and most importantly a proper fringe trim. Now this was the 70s, the golden age of what could only be described as "mum cuts" or worse, the infamous "bowl cut". A tragic fate met by many a child at the hands of the kitchen scissors, resulting in lopsided fringes so wonky you'd think Picasso had a hand in it. And if it happened to coincide with school photo week? Well, that was just the universe having a good laugh at your expense.

Luckily for me, Renee was a woman who ensured I wouldn't suffer such disgrace – no garden shears allowed.

Little did we know back then, she was delivering the finest sales pitch of her life. Between her stories of running her own salon and balancing it all with family life, she was subtly planting the seed of hairdressing wisdom.

> One day, Renee invited me into her vintage salon.

It was attached to the front of her house, giving it a curb-side appeal for the locals. It looked as if it were frozen in time since she'd retired. Breathing in the dusty scent, (still sitting on the shelves) resonated with love, I marvelled at the groundbreaking idea of entering a workspace within your own home, and within walking distance of the kettle. This practical yet artistic revelation made complete sense to me.

Her lifelong career in hairdressing explained her fiery red hair she maintained well into her 60s. She kept up on her roots, no grey allowed… Her setting rollers were diligently applied on a weekly basis to achieve stylish waves which complemented her blue eyes and pale skin. It was like her hair was a flag of defiance against time itself, matching her spirit and energy.

Standing in the salon, surrounded by echoes of a bygone era, I couldn't help but dream of having my own feather sofa of the highest quality.

In this quaint relic of a salon, a bright spark ignited within me, fuelled by the allure of creativity, the dream of a luxurious future, and the tantalising prospect of one day being my own boss.

3

DOWN UNDER

MEN AT WORK

NOW, let's rewind to the very beginning.

Brisbane, Australia, the sun-kissed cradle, is where my journey began. A tale spun by an English mum and an Irish dad, Bernadette, and Mathew, who decided to chase the promise of a new life in the Land Down Under during the early 1960s. The sun, it seemed, had a knack for shining almost all the time.

With a grand marketing drive, Australia lured skilled workers with a film reel showcasing the dreamy life on its sunny beaches - a land of endless opportunity. For a mere ten pounds, families and the like-minded could embark on an ocean voyage by ship. After six weeks at sea, welcoming transit accommodation awaited you on the other side as a stepping stone until you ventured to your chosen destination.

My parents, with two preschool daughters in tow, decided this was an opportunity too good to pass up. Everything considered, they packed their worldly belongings, keenly aware this may be a one-way ticket into the unknown. Both hailed from large families, my dad one of twelve children, my mum one of five. Bound by an era where self-discipline and independence were the bedrock of success, they bid farewell to their roots, setting sail for a new life bathed in Southern Hemisphere warmth.

Arriving in Australia, they made beachfront living a permanent fixture. They carved out a life on the esplanade in Manly, Queensland. A stark contrast to the North of England's cold confines that kept people indoors for several months of the year. My dad, a crane driver, brought his invaluable skills to the development of much-needed highways along the East Coast, while Mum, a Registered Nurse, navigated her shifts around family life – this was the dynamic duo.

Days in the Sunshine State centred around school life, community gatherings, and Catholic mass on Sundays, where Sunday best was non-negotiable.

At this time, two more daughters joined the clan, and I, as child number four, became the youngest.

In the vibrant streets of 1960s Australia, my elder sisters and the neighbourhood kids roamed freely, their days filled with endless adventures under the sun and the semi-tropical rain showers. Bullying was a foreign concept, as children were deeply ingrained into a tight-knit social fabric.

With parents enforcing strict rules, children often kept their escapades to themselves. Spin the bottle was the game-du jour, a thrilling gamble where the fateful rotation determined your next daring feat.

Picture this: the bottle spins, comes to a halt and its neck is ominously pointing at you. Your heart races as you brace for the challenge ahead. Usually a 'dare' to venture into a garden, plucking fruit hastily whilst staying under the radar of detection, then hurling the loot over the hedge for your gang to devour.

Years later, it came to light – the local retired folk found solace in attending to fruit trees, a pastime that turned the neighbourhood into a treasure trove of oranges and mangoes intended for the kids to scavenge at their will.

Weekends were a whirlwind of activity, starting early in the morning and ending late evening with a brief lunch break in between. Fridays couldn't roll around fast enough for the eagerly awaited whopping twenty cents of pocket money, which transformed into a juicy hamburger from the local corner café. Every bite a treat.

My sister Angie harboured aspirations of owning a surfboard with a price tag of seven dollars. A lofty dream, given her meagre weekly allowance. It may as well have been a trip to the moon. Crunching the numbers, the prospect of saving for anything was futile – saving a dollar required a gruelling five weeks, a surfboard, a distant dream at thirty-five weeks, a daunting eight months away.

Luckily, the benevolence and infinite wisdom of local truck drivers proved to be an alternative but creative solution. Their generous offering of tyre inner tubes served as the poor kids' floatation device, transforming water escapades into buoyant adventures.

Another dream she held was fuelled by the vision of Cat Stevens - the popular 1960s folk/pop music star, melodically strumming away on the television. The closest she got to her makeshift guitar – a mere piece of wood with elastic strings, demonstrating her determination despite its lack of musical prowess.

Once home, the evening rituals included supper and a shower, followed by the iconic TV show, "Skippy the Bush Kangaroo". Though, generally speaking, television held little allure for a population that preferred the great outdoors.

As the fourth child, I was the baby. With a five-year age gap to the next youngest of the crew, I ran behind the pack and was mothered mostly by child number two, Angela. Spending days home alone and dreaming of kindergarten, I occupied myself and became quite the explorer.

> The backyard was my private oasis

whilst my siblings attended school. My most cherished possession was an old white porcelain bathtub, repurposed as my personal pool. I spent countless hours splashing away the days under Queensland's sweltering sun. Placed squarely in the middle of the lawn at the back of the house, it offered the perfect vantage point for Mum to keep a watchful eye on me.

My hosepipe was always within easy reach to top up the water. It was my soul sanctuary. I skipped wearing shoes, embracing thongs, the national shoe of Australia, which saved us from the searing pavement heat, hot enough to fry an egg. My sisters constantly complained there were never enough pairs to go around. The scarcity of this open-toed salvation was apparent on our trips to the beach and watching them bunny hop across the sands. This involved throwing pieces of newspaper ahead of each other in a stepping stone style till they reached the edge of the surf.

In the 1960s, the Australian classroom within a religious primary school was indeed a place for learning. Obedience reigned supreme and the faintest distraction would allow you a single warning before you earned a wrap on the knuckles with a ruler. Upon arrival at the school playground, children lined up like tiny, reluctant inmates in a chain gang, their left hand dutifully perched on the shoulders of the adjacent child. This created the perfect space before dropping the arm to their side in readiness for the National Anthem to fire up.

It was, as my sister quipped, a crash course in national identity, with a strict Catholic ethos to boot. She felt this routine was designed to encourage newcomers to establish pride in their new country. Who knew this school regime would be the first example of social distancing? My sister's teachers were nuns, ranging from sweet-faced novices to stern-faced enforcers straight out of a British colonial drama. Sister Act meets Shawshank Redemption, if you will, the Reverend Mother, especially being someone the kids were keen to avoid. And woe betide any child caught uttering the forbidden "toilet" word – permission had to be earned through the sacred ritual of a raised hand a whispered request to leave the room.

But once the bell tolled for playtime, shoes were flung aside as kids raced to the playground, barefoot and free. Lunch was brought from home in a small brown case known as a "port", supplemented by the tuck-shops fresh baked cakes, where my mum helped in the rotation of volunteers. Water could be accessed from the bubblers around the school – those quirky drinking fountains that seemed to squirt water either at your face or in a gentle fountain just short of your mouth.

Playground pleasures came in the form of Knuckle Jacks, a reaction game of pick up and catching the tiny plastic jacks requiring dexterity and focus. Then there were elastics, a delightful mash-up of skipping and cat's cradle but for the feet. It involved threading a loop of elastic around the feet of two players while a third jumped in and out, weaving intricate patterns and praying not to trip over. These were the simple pleasures of the playground, which didn't require batteries, screens, or parental warnings.

Living next to the beach, a mandatory weekly swimming lesson in Manly pool was included in the curriculum. To be thrown in at the deep end, armed with nothing but a stick-shaped floatie, was a splashy baptism of sorts. The kids learned quickly how to tread water – so the objective was accomplished.

As for Sunday mass, it was less a spiritual awakening and more of a long-winded shuffle to the dreaded confessional box – as the children exchanged clueless glances for 'sin' suggestions. How were a bunch of clean-living youngsters supposed to drum up enough wrongdoing to warrant even a Hail Mary, let alone an entire rosary? Ironically, inventive fibbing to the priest became the order of the day, the real 'sin'.

Eight years in Brisbane laid the foundation for our next adventure. My dad's work led us to the stunning beaches of Bagara in the north. More importantly, known as the home of Bundy Rum.

> Kelly's Beach with its serene inlet welcomed my first set of water wings,

marking my solo entry into the warm sea. I was now a swimmer! I had also enrolled in kindergarten, another step to independence and expanding my social circle.

Bundaberg being on the edge of the tropics brought new experiences. Sugarcane and Sarsaparilla excited my tastebuds, and the scent of ripened mangos tucked in a drawer still lingers in my childhood recollections. The ever-present heat magnified the smell of zinc sunscreen and watermelon, the unmistakable fragrance of every Australian beach.

Amidst the tranquil mood of our Queenslander-style home perched on stilts, one fateful day remains etched on my brain. Our dad's well-intentioned gift to us was a glimpse of nature's wonders. Nestled beneath the house's rafters were some newly hatched chicks. Dad had monitored the nest, which had been there for some time. He decided that a quick sneak preview while the mummy bird was away gathering food for her newborns was a rare opportunity to create a lasting memory with us.

As he collected the nest and descended the ladders, we waited in anticipation, as we could hear the chirping of the baby birds. Only, Dad was unaware of the imminent danger, a ginger stray cat that roamed the neighbourhood, lurking in the shadows underneath the house.

Before we could revel in the marvels of life, tragedy struck as the cat pounced on the nest with ferocity. In a frenzy of feathers and blood, the cat's savage onslaught left us in shock, the air filled with screams and tears as the innocent chicks met their untimely demise.

My dad, feeling guilty and horrified, scurried us back into the house to our mum to guard us from the carnage.

My mum was furious that he had let this happen, the trauma for all involved and the for the poor mother bird returning to an empty nest.

Little did we know, the ginger cat harboured new life within, soon birthing a litter of five kittens beneath our home – a big surprise and twist of fate that would bind us to their care – albeit begrudgingly.

As Mum's disapproval lingered for this cat with its untamed spirit, we accepted the responsibility of nurturing them by giving them names –

> Tiger, Sunshine, Big Eyes, Smokey and Thingy Bob.

From afar, Mum observed the plight of the stray cat feeling a sense of empathy, recognising her own struggles as a mother and the need for support. Watching her tend to her kittens, her vulnerability laid bare, Mum knew she was hungry, scraping by and simply trying to survive.

But despite that understanding, my mother never warmed to cats.

Maybe it was the memory of that chaotic day when the ginger stray wreaked havoc under the house, or perhaps she just preferred dogs.

My early flashbacks of Aussie life span between the age of two to four years old, albeit, my memories are now quite sketchy. I remember sitting in my buggy outside a sweet shop shaded from the sun. My mum's friend Rosie approached me with a kind smile and slipped a bracelet onto my tiny wrist. It was made of pastel-coloured squares on elastic, but to me, it was the prettiest thing I had ever been given. That simple, charming gift ignited a lifelong adoration for bracelets.

My memories live more in essence – walking to the beach, hearing the music of that era and watching the way the sun danced on the water. Like a goldfish swimming around a bowl, my kiddie brain sat in that carefree existence. Sometimes it still does.

Life in Oz had its shades of perfection, but the relentless heat and no air conditioning lost its lustre for Mum over time. Add to that Dad's affinity for whisky and beer, and the Aussie culture for rendezvous at drinking holes presented a set of circumstances that Mum found challenging.

> As the early 70s painted Australia in a primitive scene compared to modern England,

the final blow came with the loss of both my grandmothers.

Overseas communication echoed through telegrams and letters, each word carrying the weight of miles. Candles were lit in churches and prayers were offered. Flying home for funerals was out of the question – distance and expense made it impossible. My sisters' vivid memory of our mum kneeling in church with her head in her hands and weeping revealed the depths of her despair. It was a moment that marked the lowest ebb, and a grief too heavy to conceal. She had painstakingly saved a nest egg over the years in the hope of returning to England. The impact of our family's loss hit my mum the hardest. With her dad now in an English nursing home, her desire to return and care for him grew stronger by the day. It was like a magnet pulling her back to familiar territory.

> The yearning for South Yorkshire's close-knit communities and bustling high streets surged.

The battle ensued, and Mum emerged victorious. And, just like that, Dad reluctantly relinquished his ties to the Australian dream.

With our inevitable departure, the cat and her kittens were sent away to live on a farm, marking the bittersweet conclusion to our tumultuous encounter with the ginger stray. Well, that was the story we were told!

After a decade of outdoor adventures as Aussie kids, our Antipodean adventure faded as we boarded the plane for England.

4

ON ILKLEY MOOR BAHT' 'AT
SILKSTONE BRASS BAND

ARRIVING in England after hopping across multiple continents on a string of plane connections, the first thing that hit me was the chill in the air and the organised chaos of a London bus station. At four and a half, I found myself wearing proper clothes for the first time. Let me tell you, dungarees, a jumper and real shoes felt like an existential itchy crisis compared to my usual carefree attire.

It was April 1973, and after a whirlwind introduction to British weather, we soon found ourselves in the North of England, in particular the grand county of Yorkshire. As if it could get any colder.

My earliest memory in this new world involved being perched on the kitchen countertop, munching on a raspberry jam sandwich. The radio transmitted the same songs in the sunny land we'd just left – Lynn Anderson's "Rose Garden" which to this day is my happy song and takes me back to that jam sandwich feeling.

Along with other hits from the Bee Gees, Neil Diamond, and the very popular Pushbike Song, this harmonious presence of familiar tunes helped me adapt to this newfound land.

This was the first time I truly felt my mum's presence so strongly. Perhaps it was the fact I was now indoors with her in our cosy two-up, two-down, house. Previously, my domain had always been outdoors. My sisters were now enrolled in school and dad was at work. This new but temporary space was our rental as we searched for a larger home to fit six people plus Grandad.

I was looking forward to meeting Grandad, though it was bittersweet for Mum as Grandma had died four years earlier. My grandad was Irish, an ex-miner, a proper, no-nonsense tailgate ripper, who'd dedicated his life to battling coal seams at the pit face. Years of slogging away underground had earned him a handshake from the Queen and a hefty dose of pneumoconiosis. The mining life might have filled his pockets, but it sure took the wind out of his lungs.

By the time I came into the picture, the disease had slowed him down to a shuffle and landed him in a nursing home, unable to live on his own. Mum had always had a warm, close bond with her Dad, the kind of man who rolled his sleeves up and prioritised family life and his role as a husband.

Mum, deciding to marry an Irishman, probably assumed she was signing up for a similar deal, but instead of maintaining the equilibrium, Dad seemed to be increasingly knocking it off its axis. I think Mum secretly hoped Grandad's calm, steady presence might sprinkle some much-needed decorum back into her life. Only decorum isn't contagious, and Matty wasn't about to be infected by good behaviour anytime soon.

At least, now back on home soil, Mum could hunt for that family home to scoop us all back together under one roof, and this new base was the starting point.

> This quaint little house came with a front garden and a backyard, complete with an outdoor loo and a coal house.

It was snug and despite its lack of luxury, it was functional and simple – much like my new wardrobe.

My first time venturing out into this shared backyard was an easy transition. A few children my age invited me to turn bricks over to find earwigs and beetles. This was a new branch of nature to me.

It didn't take long for the neighbourhood to catch wind of the Australian kids' arrival, creating a bit of a buzz. Soon enough, we had friends galore.

Ann was my first English friend. She was a bit of a tomboy, with short brown hair, green eyes, and an infectious laugh. One day, she appeared at the door with a straightforwardness only a five-year-old can muster.

> "Wanna come out to play?"

We'd go swimming and make up ridiculous dance routines, and her dog, Chance, was always on hand to terrorise the neighbourhood kids with a cheeky growl or an opportunistic nip. Back then, the streets buzzed with kids of all ages, running riot and playing outside because everyone lived practically on top of each other. We'd turn the nearby allotments into our personal playground, crafting obstacle courses straight out of some unhinged adventure film—pure, unfiltered childhood anarchy. There was always that one kid with a "fancy" digital watch, timing us as we tore through the circuit, leaping off garages onto saggy old mattresses that probably had more life stories than we did. Our parents? They had no clue. And maybe that was for the best...

It was the 70s, so this was the ultimate social invitation. A simple knock on the door was all it took to spark a new adventure. I accepted, grabbed my shoes and buckled them up with enthusiasm as this felt like the beginning of something new and exciting. Little did I know, this was the beginning of a lifelong friendship. Fast forward thirteen years, and there she was, still my partner in crime, except this time, she was sitting in my salon chair, trusting me with her hair for a Colour trophy competition. Spoiler alert: I won. But it wasn't the trophy that was priceless – it was knowing I had a friend for life who didn't mind being a guinea pig for my hairdressing ambitions.

Fifty years later, we're still thick as thieves, even though we live on opposite sides of the globe. Ann lives in the United States, and I'm in Australia, but thank the tech gods for social media. It's like we're living next door again. Whether it's a quick message or a two-hour phone call, we pick up right where we left off. Old friends really are the best. There's something about being linked by hearts and humour that makes time and distance irrelevant. But heaven help if we ever end up in the same nursing home. We would have to be kept under a special watch.

But let's hope that adventure is still a way off. In the meantime, we've got big plans – a Honky-Tonk bar tour around America. We just know there's a mechanical bull somewhere out there with our name on it, just begging to throw us off in style.

Back then, in the early 70's, when we were five years old. Our version of high-octane thrills involved juggling as many balls as possible against a wall in rotation, mastering the art of a hula hoop like our hips depended on it, and collecting glass marbles like they were crown jewels, every colour under the sun. Simpler times when life's biggest dilemma revolved around whether to throw the marble or nudge it. We were living life on the edge, folks, living on the edge.

Sundays brought a new routine: a new church and a new Parish to meet. Now that was just down the street, but soon enough, I started primary school. Naturally, it was a Catholic school, but not the one on our doorstep – Oh no. My mum, ever the education crusader, insisted we all went to schools outside our local area. Her reasoning? To ensure we were surrounded by good role models and a solid Catholic environment.

The upside? We got to have a whole separate set of school friends from home friends, which, in kid logic, meant twice the fun and half the trouble.

My school had an extra special selling point! A headmistress – who was a nun, backed by a chorus of guitar-playing nuns. Because why not?

The school itself looked like it was plucked from a postcard, surrounded by green fields and conveniently served as a feeder school for the secondary school where my elder sisters were already laying down the law. At the grand age of five, I embarked on a daily four-mile bus ride that was my first taste of independence. Sister number three was my travel companion for the first term, after that, she would move on to high school, and I was going it alone.

I still remember my first day. My mum, playing her part, took me to class – an event that would happen only once. I was assigned to a buddy named Sharon who greeted me with a smile. I plopped down on the mat next to her, and just like that, my school life began.

By the end of the day, my Aussie accent had earned me the unimaginative nickname, Aussie.

Now, these guitar-slinging nuns were a far cry from the fire-and-brimstone Aussie nuns my sisters had warned me about. No, these nuns were kind and patient, strumming away like they were rehearsing for Nunstock. To my young, naive mind, they weren't nuns so much as sisters who'd opted for the convent's all-inclusive package – peace and quiet, and no husband to nag them about misplaced socks.

This new environment ignited my love of ABCs, story time on the mat, and the rows of dusty, dog-eared books on the class shelf. But the real treasure was the opulent dressing-up box in the corner, bursting with an array of beautiful gowns. I couldn't wait for the bell to ring 'twice', signalling it was a rainy playtime – which let's face it, was often – so I could race and grab my favourite gold gown before anyone else. If I didn't scramble fast enough to nab my first choice, I'd graciously settle for the magenta gown. The rain might have been bucketing down, but inside, I was royalty, reigning supreme over my imaginary kingdom, all while maintaining my dignity.

> Well, as much as one could, being a five-year-old with sticky fingers and a crooked paper crown.

Moving from Australia to Yorkshire was like jumping into a time machine and landing smack in the middle of the Holy Land – at least that's how it felt to our ears. Back in Australia, the only English accents we heard were the crisp, Queen's English types and from watching war films on the telly. So, when we arrived at a Yorkshire school where everyone sounded like they were narrating the Old Testament, we were all truly gobsmacked.

Angela came home after her first day, wide-eyed and convinced that she'd stumbled into the most devout population since the days of Moses. "They're all deeply religious," she announced, fretting over how she'd ever manage to understand, or worse, communicate with these new-found disciples. Turns out, the school was less strict than she feared, but cracking the code of the South Yorkshire / Barnsley language would be her new divine challenge.

In Yorkshire, questions weren't just questions; they were riddles wrapped in an accent that seemed to come with its own dictionary. Phrases and grammar were twisted in ways that left us laughing one minute and scratching our heads the next. And don't get me started on the use of the word "the" — it's like it's gone on holiday and never come back.

As for me, I was too young to be phased by this linguistic puzzle. If anything, I thought the whole thing was a bit of a lark. Plus, I had an ace up my sleeve – an Irish Dad with an accent so thick you could spread it on toast. Thanks to him, my ears were already trained for this kind of nonsense, so I didn't even notice if I had an accent myself.

So, there we were, navigating our way through the Yorkshire dialect, one indecipherable sentence at a time.

Fortunately, Angela was practically a child prodigy when it came to education, which came in handy when tackling the Yorkshire dialect. Making new friends was supposed to be the easy part, or so she thought.

She'd come home with her daily report, breaking down the lingo.

Today someone asked me, *"What's thi name?"* (What's your name?) she'd say, as if recounting a conversation with a long-lost relative from Mars. Then she'd hit us with,

> *"Weer tha frum? Wiz tha been? 'n' Weer atha goin?"*

(Where are you from? Where have you been? And, where are you going?).

The poor girl was trying to decipher a new language on the fly, and her brain was working overtime just to keep up.

On top of all that, mornings were a fast-paced routine to catch the school bus. Four frantic people, each battling to get out of the door simultaneously. It was a game of "Find the shoes," "Where's the bag," and "Who's moved my gym kit?" Our house was like a TARDIS, a compact space that contained everything except what you were looking for.

One memorable morning, I was halfway to the bus stop when it hit me: I had forgotten to put my knickers on. Absolute panic set in. I legged it back up my street like my life depended on it, one hand gripping my skirt to keep it from giving everyone a free show. My brain was in full meltdown mode – thoughts of missing the bus, being late for registration, and the sheer horror of facing a nun, and me with no knickers. I was too young and innocent to even attempt a white lie, especially to a nun. They can sense that stuff. That sprint home taught me the importance of organization: I learned to be punctual and prepared and to have all the essentials— foundations for my future as a hairdresser. You can't survive a day at school, or anywhere else, without the right tools. Or knickers.

It wasn't long before my parents bought a house just around the corner. Finally, a place to house six people. Yay!

It came with its own title plaque on the brickwork next to the front door, "Leyland House". This grand villa-style house boasted three floors and a basement cellar nestled within a walled garden. The garden had mature apple and cherry trees, winding pathways for adventures, and even an outdoor loo.

Moving house was an ordeal that brought the whole neighbourhood out in force. Picture, if you will, a circus of suitcases, wheelbarrows, and any contraptions we could utilise to move one hundred metres down the road. No car, just an army of families transporting handheld items, worker-ant style, back and forth. The 1970s were like that – people were happy to lend a hand, and in one day we went from a tiny box to a sprawling space. Ann helped – she carried a lampshade, wearing the shade as a hat.

The rooms were enormous, each with its own open fireplace, which was essential given the single-glazed windows and Yorkshire's bone-chilling winters. The sash-style bedroom windows were perfect for my nimble little body to climb through, not to shimmy down the drainpipe, but to make a branching stretch onto the wash house extension at the rear of the house.

This rooftop became my special sunbathing spot with a view over the neighbouring vegetable allotments. They were laid out in a grid, like a mini ecosystem. Chickens laying eggs, turkeys being reared for Christmas, and cockerels providing the dawn chorus.

> Add the sweet bird song and the perfume of apple blossoms. My childhood felt like an endless summer of possibilities. The name of the street is very apt.

SUMMER LANE

My favourite room was the attic, entered by a swing door on the third floor. Its previous history – a well-renowned business as a ballet school.

A majestic room which scaled the length of the house, still complete with mirrored walls and ballet bars. With no dance teacher in sight, I chose gymnastics, self-taught, of course. This runway in the apex of the top floor was a true hidden gem where I could explore and let my imagination run wild.

The polished timber floors had just the right amount of traction, especially when paired with cushions for a soft landing. Watching Nadia Comaneci on television sparked my love for gymnastics. Her approach to each piece of apparatus had me glued to the television. I was drawn to her gracefulness and open body language, which seemed so feminine.

Her floor routines were a masterclass in elegance, with every movement meticulously arranged, flowing seamlessly into a solid round-off and a flawless landing. I needed to emulate her grace – to stretch and lengthen my limbs, to mirror her poise, to find my version of controlled movement within this art.

Maybe it was my knack for climbing trees or just pure agility, but as a kid, I was soon bending my body into any shape I wished. This sporty girl was a budding gymnast and could not be contained. All I needed was space.

> I fancied myself quite the bohemian artiste, with long flowing hair – never mind that my "hair" was a pair of ladies' tights slapped on my head.

The body shaper was my makeshift cap, with the legs hanging down to mimic lengthy locks. Who could resist a pair of ten deniers in American tan? Never mind that mum could never find a pair to wear for work.

Overall, it was a quirky dream house with the ultimate playground: various trees to climb and my sun deck on the wash house roof – a paradise for my adventurous spirit. My dad, clearly a man of vision, dubbed me "monkey" for my uncanny ability to balance along high walls like a mini-Olympian and scale tree branches as if I had a secret plan to reach the moon.

To honour my parkour prowess, he installed a rope swing from the cherry tree, expertly positioned for optimal swing space. That tree became my kingdom, a leafy fortress with a built-in snack bar! I was now a branch manager. I devoured juicy cherries, grabbing them before the birds feasted.

The tree was conveniently entwined with an apple tree, so I had a dual fruit option, all within arm's reach. To this day, I can't pass a mature tree without eyeing it like an old friend, mentally mapping out the best route to climb it. Some people see trees as just part of the landscape – I see them as an open invitation to relive my childhood glory days.

5

LIFE IN A NORTHERN TOWN
DREAM ACADEMY

GROWING UP IN THE 70S, the meals were as thrilling as watching paint dry. The standard fare? Meat and two veg – about as adventurous as a stroll around a cul-de-sac, unless you were lucky enough to discover the delightful culinary comestibles Staniforth's bakery had on offer.

At home, the family kitchen was where innovation meant adding a sprinkle of salt to some potatoes. My weekly trip to the bakery was the equivalent of a Michelin-star experience for a pup like me. My routine with my mum was a trot onto the high street, first visiting the library, then onwards for my favourite treat. I was a predictable little creature. Every visit, I'd order a ham salad sandwich, a gingerbread man, and a glass of milk, the height of sophistication.

Over the years, I've bravely expanded my horizons, working my way through Stanis' entire menu, but there's one treat that will always hold my tastebuds hostage. The rhubarb and custard tart. It's pure hypnosis in pastry form. If I ever make it onto Mastermind, my specialist subject would be "Staniforths Bakery – 1973-2020". No passes or tiebreakers needed.

My sixth birthday party was a grand affair, celebrated in our new house with a sprawling garden that felt like it went on forever. The highlight? Gorging on Staniforth's trifles, of course. Back in the 70s, we ate with the reckless abandon of people who knew they would burn calories as soon as we inhaled them. There was no such thing as too much sugar and portion control. Not a bother. Sometimes you got more, sometimes less, and the food was the food.

As my birthday party wound down, Ann and I commandeered the front room, crafting our own top-notch choreography to the gift she had bought me. A seven-inch vinyl record single of the huge smash hit, "Kung Fu Fighting" by Carl Douglas. We played it on a loop, spinning the vinyl until the needle wore out. To this day, whenever those opening lyrics hit, we both drop into our original karate stance, as if we're ready to take on Bruce Lee himself.

My mum was, shall we say, an "adequate" cook – a title she'd happily accept if she didn't have to fry another pork chop. Still, she had a nose for the best quality staples. Fish and chips were our fast food and always within walking distance. The greasy, golden aroma emanating from the chippy doorway captivated and drew me in. And if we were feeling wildly adventurous, we could opt for a Chinese takeaway. Back then, ordering sweet and sour pork was as exotic as backpacking through the Himalayas. The Chinese immigrants, knowing they had a tough crowd to please, wisely numbered the dishes on the menu, just in case we Brits fumbled with the pronunciations. Thank God for the sweet simplicity of "Number 37 with egg fried rice."

Ironically, it's the same with hair colour charts. Just like we needed help to order chow mein, hairdressers breathe a sigh of relief when they can rely on numbers. Sure, we can all remember the trusty base shades – they are our daily bread. But give us an unusual funky red, copper, or an obscure plum shade, and we're stumped.

> "Oh, you mean number 66|46? That's um ... reddish, right?"

It's like we never left that Chinese takeaway; numbers are still the universal language.

Back in the day, when the weather allowed, kids were feral in the best possible way. We spent every waking hour outdoors, riding our bikes and roller skates from dawn till dusk, and I simply ran behind the pack. Traffic was light, apart from the occasional milk float and the odd neighbour driving their car majestically at fifteen miles per hour.

And of course, we had that one kid on the block with the fancy racer bike who would speed past us all with a smug grin, but we ignored him, naturally. Even when I was restricted to the garden, there was always my Heinz 57 variety, dog – an affectionate term for a mutt of no specific breed, who was always up for a game of "chase your own tail." On rainy days, I'd sit with a colouring book, surrounded by felt-tip pens and line up my dolls for their "hair appointments." I'd meticulously brush their synthetic locks, deciding who to scalp first.

People routinely set Sundays aside for family time in the 1970s, whether you liked it or not. No one bothered asking if you had other plans, because, frankly, you didn't. The world collectively sighed and embarked on endless house chores, a day observed like an unspoken ritual. The kids were roped into it too, probably to keep us from killing each other out of boredom.

We would all be up to our elbows doing laundry, tossing whites and colours into the twin-tub machine as if feeding some rabid beast. By lunchtime, the house smelt of roast beef and damp socks, which somehow felt comforting.

> Sunday lunch was a serious affair – usually involving meat cooked within an inch of its life,

mashed potatoes with lumps big enough to trip over, and boiled-to-death veg, but at least the Yorkshire puddings and gravy saved the day.

Meanwhile, the dads were in the garden, pretending to "relax" by mowing lawns and washing cars, all whilst lecturing us how "Sundays' were meant to be the day of rest." One neighbour meticulously polished his Ford Cortina, as though expecting a surprise visit from the Queen. They'd lean on the fence, chatting about sport, politics, and petrol prices, all while secretly judging each other's hedges.

And if you were unlucky, they'd drag you off to church, where the priest would drone on about the virtues of patience, which was ironic considering every kid in the pews was praying for a quick exit.

Now, if any of my friends made the mistake of calling round on a Sunday, my mum would immediately draft them into the Bernadette Crusade. My mum had this uncanny ability to connect with her inner John the Baptist and convert any unsuspecting mate into an honorary Catholic with one guilt-inducing look. So off they'd come to mass with us, looking shell-shocked – but too polite to refuse. To this day, those same friends insist they're "a little bit Catholic," thanks to Bernadette's unshakeable influence.

Sundays were predictable, tedious, and somehow sacred in their own weird working-class way. By teatime, the day finally wound down, leaving you staring at the telly with a belly full of Yorkshire pudding, waiting for Monday to roll around so you could escape the house and get back to school.

My mum, a night shift Nurse, was also taking care of Grandad, who now had his permanent residence in his armchair next to the fire in the front room. She had it all sorted, or so it seemed. She had achieved her goals, and it was time to unpack some boxes she had overlooked. They had been buried in the rear of a closet and unopened since our move from Australia. In the rummage, she discovered some identifying documents.

> "Oh, by the way, you're not born on August 28th anymore; you're born on the 23rd,"

she said as if she was informing me we were out of tea. Apparently, the 28th was the day she walked out of the hospital with me. So, like any dutiful eight-year-old daughter, I waddled into school and told my teacher my birthday had been relocated, who couldn't hide her confused smirk. She was naturally curious as I explained that my birth certificate had been MIA. I can only imagine how that story made its rounds in the staffroom, complete with snorts of laughter and raised eyebrows. I was used to my mum's slight degree of scattiness, and who could blame her with such an active and demanding brood?

The real trauma for me was moving my birth sign from Virgo to the cusp of Leo / Virgo, creating an astrological identity crisis. Over the years, it has always been a great conversation starter when I meet someone with that same birthday. I'd chime in, "Oh, that used to be my birthday too," and watch their faces contort into confusion before they inevitably beg for an explanation.

To this day, I still feel like I deserve two birthdays like Queen Elizabeth. After all, I am named after her.

6

DEVIL'S HAIRCUT

BECK

EMBARKING on a forty-year hairdressing odyssey has been a wild ride through four decades of learning. Or, as I like to call it, the never-ending quest for follicular enlightenment. Now let me take you back to the roots – pun intended – where it all began.

In the world of hairdressing, your first clients are typically the brave souls from within your circle, namely family and friends. These unsuspecting victims, I mean volunteers, willingly step into the chair of uncertainty, waiting to face whatever experimental artistry awaits.

My hair has always been a bit of an identity crisis – not quite curly, not quite straight. A shade of light brown that could be described as "boring" and deciding not to participate. My journey was born out of a personal mission to wrangle my own unruly locks and find excitement in the vast world of hairstyles and fashion.

My hair has an ongoing feud with a red undertone. The bleaching process it endures is nothing short of akin to a strawberry blonde battle, demanding the level of patience usually reserved for teaching cats to dance the cha-cha.

Yet this battle has equipped me with the skills to tackle colour corrections and the aftermath of box dye debacles with the level of confidence that only comes from surviving countless hair-related skirmishes.

Let me regale you with the tale of my first plunge into the hair perming jungle. The popular perm style of the time was the bubble cut – a short curly perm designed for a no-fuss afro comb and air dry. Marketers promoted it as the ultimate low-maintenance curl. Amusingly, people would ask their hairdresser for that "bubble cut", as if a pair of enchanted scissors would snip hair into perfect curls. The reality was a lot less magical of course. It involved rows of perm rods and chemical solutions, going heavy on the ammonia and light on the fairy dust. If only it was that easy.

> Picture it: the '80s, a time of wild experimentation and questionable fashion choices.

A friend with a short 'bob' hairstyle, dared me to perm her hair at home. Now, I wasn't a seasoned stylist back then, just a fearless experimenter with a questionable understanding of perming. Armed with a perming kit and a head full of misguided confidence, I set out on what would become my best and worst perming adventure.

The instructions on the box were my guiding light, or so I thought. I delicately sectioned and wrapped the fragile ends of her hair around the uniform blue plastic rods, secured them in place and applied the solution. Rod size versus hair length? Quality solution? Pfft, who cared back then? Waiting for the magic to happen, we blissfully hoped for the best, unaware that hair destiny was about to unfold.

After the rinsing and neutralising ritual, the unveiling began. Each curl sprang to life like it had a vendetta against gravity and nowhere more crucial than the fringe. My friends' eyes searched uphill as each curl stubbornly sprang into tight little coils on her forehead, her fringe clearly on a sabbatical. No amount of coaxing with an afro comb could tame the rebellion.

The result was hardly a shocker, considering the plan was more "wing it," than "well thought out." As I handed her the mirror, my mind was already halfway out the door, mentally rehearsing my escape line – "Wow, look at the time. "Gotta dash!"

As her new look finally came into focus, the bewilderment on her face matched mine perfectly.

This experiment, my friends resulted in a paradox – the best perm ever because it took like a champ, and the worst because it turned my friend into a teenage version of Art Garfunkel.

> Not so much, Scarborough fair. Rather, "Sorry about your hair!"

Imagine the shock, followed by laughter, as we contemplated the unforeseen masterpiece. And so, we learned the timeless lesson.

Sometimes, a perm to fix and straighten a perm is the lesser evil when faced with Art Garfunkel comparisons from high school peers. Thankfully, a perm solution is a bit of a double agent. It can tighten a curl or loosen it up, depending on what side you need it on. So, with the current disaster in full bloom, the only option was a mad sprint to the shop before they closed for another perm kit.

An hour later, after the daring rescue mission was complete, her fringe was back, though it required a bit of therapy. A good hydrating conditioner was about to become her best friend in the foreseeable future.

7

IT MUST HAVE BEEN LOVE
ROXETTE

I CAN'T WRITE this book without including the zany and unconventional upbringing, gifted to me by my two wonderful parents, who I can only describe as being very happy, right up until they met! How I would have loved to be a fly on the wall in the early years of their romance. I imagine it involved a lot of raised eyebrows and misunderstandings, which, I can assure you, continued throughout the marriage.

My dad came from Ireland as a young man in search of work and landed in South Yorkshire, where he met my mum. Mum. Sensing that Irish connection, her own dad being Irish – probably figured,

> 'He's Catholic, he's charming, and he's not half bad in a suit, so why not?'

Back then, the Irish lads were like the 'Boyzone' of their time, arriving in droves, suited and booted, causing a stir among the local blokes who were left clutching their pints, wondering where it all went wrong. The new arrivals had the look, the quirky humour, and the determination to succeed, which was how Dad wooed Mum – or so I imagine.

After a brief romance, Mum took a stint in the US city of Philadelphia to advance her nurse training and broaden her horizons, leaving Dad to sharpen his letter-writing skills. The young romantics kept in touch via mailed letters, and upon her return, they soon got married, ready to take on the world – or at least a small corner of South Yorkshire. They were a handsome couple, my mother sporting a copper flame of hair and my father, inky black locks.

Fast forward fourteen years and four kids later, and that picture had shifted dramatically.

> If marriage is the ultimate test of compatibility, parenthood is the final exam, the ultimate reality check.

Step forward Wilma and Fred Flintstone: not so much star-crossed lovers as weary cave dwellers grunting across the cave at each other as they claimed the Bedrock Lifestyle of the Year award.

Growing up, Dad always worked away, which suited him and Mum just fine. We were never short of money, but parenting was more of a solo act for Mum, with Dad swooping in like a visiting dignitary.

In reality, it was less "team effort" and more like an episode from the classic old British comedy, Steptoe and Son with a turnstile down the middle of the house. Dad would roll in after six weeks away, and the first to greet him would be Jip the dog – who went berserk. I'm talking full-on canine hysteria, with the dog charging at him with a 2 x 4 plank of wood, like they were about to start a round of mediaeval jousting. The dog's shrieks and jumps were heartwarming, a display only a pet can muster when reunited with a beloved missing family member.

Dad would immediately engage with the dog, offering us a cursory greeting whilst casting a sheepish glance towards Mum to gauge whether his presence was welcome. The answer was usually no. It was evident he and the dog had developed an alliance and communicated in a language known only to themselves. Before long, the lump of timber would be sailing the full length of the indoor living area, bouncing off the furniture and radiogram. Even the goldfish would duck frantically, praying they would stay in the water and live to swim another day. This boisterous game of fetch with the dog, was, I suppose, Dad's way of easing into the domestic battlefield, testing the waters with Mum – the redhead who had little patience for his shenanigans.

My mum, on the other hand, would show an exasperated sigh of low-level annoyance and mutter, "Oh, he's back, "before turning on heel and making herself scarce. Our house was big enough that everyone could find their own corner to escape to when needed.

I, however, knew my treat was coming, a fountain of coins he had saved to add to my huge whisky bell jar I'd commandeered as a piggy bank. I had no idea what I was saving for, but I was committed to the task. The coppers grew higher with each visit, and I grew more motivated for that rainy day shopping spree.

Once settled in, Dad would head out to the pub for a few pints and on his return, would reconnect with his beloved Irish vinyl. John McCormack would be blasting at full volume serenading the house with sentimental Irish ballads. Dad, swaying in time, would toast the night with a few tots of whisky.

Meanwhile, Mum would be in the adjacent room, puffing on a cigarette, drowning out John McCormack, grooving to Barry White and all the Motown hits. Crossing that threshold within my home was a musical journey onto its own, a persistent war of tenor and tambourine. Neither were going to enter the other's patch.

It was always great to have the family together, but chaos was never far off. And Dad never disappointed.

Friends, family, and visitors to the house always found my mum and dads' relationship a great source of amusement. Unlike the ordinary or mundane households of their own, daily life in our house was more like a sitcom.

My mum, a nurse who worked permanently on the night shift, raising four children, kept things straightforward and no nonsense. Dad, however, would come home every six weeks and inevitably bring his own brand of havoc. Or maybe he was just somewhat crushed under the acute concentration of females in one domicile. My parents' legendary bickering became the go-to entertainment for anyone needing a good laugh, and on occasion we the children would join in.

Dad, in his own charmingly chaotic way, would try to endear himself to her, but Mum knew any chance of a peaceful and pleasant time would be short lived as Matty's own unique brand of unintentional sabotage was just around the corner.

Outside nursing and family life, Bernadette dreamed of modern luxury and travel. Matty, raised on a farm in Ireland, was more about making do and mending. Any home improvement would inevitably bear the "Matty stamp." You practically needed a "Matty manual" to operate our central heating and hot water system, a combination of a tricky clicky clock dial and a vertical lever that resembled an ice skate blade – or maybe that's what it was.

Understanding it was akin to mastering the Flux Capacitor from Back to the Future. When the system fired up with a rumble reminiscent of the DeLorean time machine, you knew you were in business. The radiators rattled, the attic water tank hissed and steamed like a content volcano. All this preparation in pursuit of a hot bath.

Dad's creativity knew no bounds. Where most people might be satisfied with a few sheets of newspaper and a match to light a fire, Dad invented a shortcut: "Why go simple when you can go spectacularly unsafe?" So, he rigged a gas poker out of a long copper pipe and a rubber hose that, somehow, he had casually hooked into the gas supply.

Visitors, who had no idea what horror they had walked into, would watch as he turned a wing nut, releasing a whoosh of gas, before striking a match. In an instant, our kitchen turned into a scene from the movie, Backdraft, complete with an open flame that would've given any fire safety inspector a nervous tic. He'd shove the makeshift flamethrower into the fireplace until the coals went from lukewarm to positively volcanic. Then he'd switch off the valve and hang the contraption on a hook next to the range, with a satisfied grin, and settle in to cook his dinner.

But not in the oven, and certainly not the stove that was just sitting there, judging him, silently. Oh no, he'd balance baked bean tins over the embers with a pair of long-handled coal tongs and proceed to cook everything from scrambled eggs to Irish stew, his rustic recipes offered to anyone brave enough to try.

In later life, his grandkids were curious but willing Guinea Pigs in his culinary experiments and remember the experiences with a mixture of fondness and bemusement, and what I can only assume is slight PTSD.

Imagine being served your dinner cooked in bean tins over coals, when there's a perfectly functioning stove over in the corner. And if you made it through dinner, you were rewarded with life lessons in his makeshift distillery - a dank little cellar where he brewed the occasional batch of homemade Potcheen. He was determined to pass down these vital Irish skills to future generations.

> Because, what's more important than knowing how to whip up a rustic meal and concoct your own moonshine?

And if you think he was only inventive when it came to cooking, you've missed half the story. The taps around the house were a masterclass in patchwork plumbing.

If a faucet broke, it was game on for dad. He'd solve the issue with whatever was within reach – pliers, rubber bands, or something he'd rigged up in his shed and whatever had survived his toolbox that week.

Any contraption you could squeeze and twist to get things flowing would do the trick. It was all part of his unique, "Matty" charm.

HAIR TRAFFIC CONTROL

One of Dads' many "projects" began innocently enough with a request from Mum asking him to fix a wobbly leg on our beloved red faux leather sofa. Not a big ask you would think. But this was the 1970s, and DIY was an extreme sport back then.

Furniture wasn't just "off the rack," and parts couldn't be bought with just a click on a keyboard. So, Dad improvised.

Mum arrived home from work to find the sofa on...... roller skates. Yes, actual wheels, all facing in the same direction. No rotation, just a straight on.

The real magic happened when unsuspecting guests would plop themselves down, only to find the room lurch beneath them as they hurtled towards the window, clutching the arm rest for dear life, convinced they were having a vertigo attack. His sofa-turned-amusement ride never failed to elicit giggles.

Dads' knack for "housekeeping" without consulting mum, led to some legendary surprises. One morning, after Mum finished a gruelling twelve hour night shift, she returned to find the kitchen pantry had gone. Not a door removed or shelf missing – no, he had demolished it.

All that remained was a pile of rubble, exposed brick, and Dad's signature touch: a bare lightbulb tacked to the wall, with a repurposed apple pie tin as a reflector, casting a blinding spotlight on the carnage. Just as quickly as he'd created this scene, he left for work, leaving Mum and her demolished pantry to marinate together for what turned out to be two full years. My mum just stared at the wreckage in the morning light, torn between hysterics and homicide.

Dad's skill set was honed from years of being raised on a farm, only he didn't have to suffer the consequences of his handiwork. Working away from home, his lifestyle was, shall we say, miles away from Mum's reality of single-handedly managing a household bursting with kids.

Meanwhile, neighbours and friends would flock to the house to gawk at Dad's latest "home improvements," like visitors at a DIY house of horrors. It was less "Grand Designs" and more "DIY SOS – but no one called for help." Meanwhile, Mum – Bernadette, the unshakeable Legend, stood in the background sipping her tea like it was holy water. If Sainthood had a fast-track application, her name would have been high up the list.

Each project had the distinct air of "You'll never believe what he's done this time." And no matter how many times we thought, surely, he can't top this, he always did.

Friends would often stop mid-stare at Dad's latest masterpiece, their faces a picture of polite horror. They'd squint, trying to make sense of the wood, nails, and sheer physical improbability in front of them before cautiously asking, "So, what exactly is that? Or what's that going to be?" The best answer? "Don't ask!" Or as we learned to say, "We don't know yet," because the odds were, neither did he.

My friends, bless them, couldn't resist the lure of the funny Irish man.

They would edge closer with curiosity and caution. "What are you making, Mr McVey?" they'd ask, watching as he hammered away at some odd timber framework which looked suspiciously close to finished.

> "Oh," he'd say with a thoughtful pause, barely glancing up, "I'm not quite sure yet, maybe a ladder for the dog."

And with that, he'd return to his hammering, leaving them smiling, giggling, and utterly baffled. Because, of course, what dog doesn't need a ladder?

The thing was, there were no limits to his quirky inventions. In his mind, he still saw himself as that farmer's lad who had been put to work at age five, always scheming "practical" solutions in his own recycled way.

So naturally, we came to be the only house – in the street, county, possibly the entire country – where every ground-floor door had low-level "patented" handles specifically for the dog. This was just our normal, as Jip glided from room to room demonstrating his push-paw technique, which had guests cocking their heads to one side. Our dog had better mobility options than most toddlers, and a better doggy pantry too.

Ah, yes, it didn't stop there. Jip the dog wasn't just a door-opening virtuoso; he was a culinary connoisseur, the master of the fine art of food rejection. You see, regular dog food was for other dogs, those less discerning, perhaps even a bit common. Tin food? Not on Jip's menu. That stuff would sit in the bowl like an unwanted guest at a party – completely ignored.

No, Jip demanded nothing but the prime cuts from the butcher, cooked fresh, daily, of course. He had standards, you see. We would carefully prepare his meals with the same dedication as a chef plating for royalty- because to be fair, Jip was the king of the castle.

His one true indulgence? Frolic dog treats. But then, it wasn't just about eating them. It would turn into a game of aerial aerobatics. We would toss a frolic into the air, and he would leap up like some kind of canine gymnast, snapping it in mid-flight. That was a workout for both parties.

> Now Jip wasn't a lone wolf, oh no. He had a best mate, Prince, who lived a few streets over.

The two of them had this adorable little routine where they'd literally call for each other to hang out. Who knew? Dogs with a social calendar. But here's the kicker: Prince didn't come over for Jip's sparkling personality. It was all about his leftovers. Prince had the look that said. "If you're not gonna eat it mate, I'm more than happy to."

And then there was mum, a night shift warrior who'd wake up in the afternoon, only to find, not one, but two dogs draped across her bed, like a couple of fuzzy throw pillows. On those cold winter nights, Prince would just stay over, leading to an inevitable exchange of phone numbers. Always handy when they decided to pull an impromptu sleepover.

And if our house wasn't already a strange museum of objet d'art for the insane, lovingly curated by 'Professor Matty', My dad never stopped creating and thinking outside the box.

Another gem in Dad's lineup of questionable inventions was his self-styled traction machine, tucked away in the attic. He'd cobbled it together from an old bike wheel, a tangle of pulleys, and a foam bandage, fashioned into a sort of noose to cradle his chin. It looked like something from a movie torture chamber– Frankenstein meets a spin class. But to him, it was a back-saver and a money-saver, a DIY chiropractor on demand.

Invitations to the attic for a live demo were a regular occurrence.

> "Come on up and see how it works!"

Dad, lying flat on the floor, one foot pushing the pedal whilst the foam noose held his head in a gentle, mediaeval chokehold. Our mum, the real nurse in our family, gave up long ago commenting on his peculiar medical practices. Early on, she'd tried the nurse route, explaining that strangling oneself wasn't recognized therapy for back pain. But Dad was undeterred, determined that this contraption would fix all his spinal woes. He'd be on the floor daily, as cheerful as ever. Just one pedal away from asphyxiation. We all learned to step around him, quite literally, as he tinkered on his unique journey to wellness.

8

FASHION

DAVID BOWIE

THE LATE 1970S and through the 1980s were a time of rapid evolution in terms of fashion, hairstyles and music. The world music scene was an exciting explosion of sonic styles and vibrant visual expression.

You could tell what someone was into by the way they strutted down the street. Their hair, their jacket, the way they flicked their cigarette, or tapped their boot – you'd think, "Oh yeah, he's a Bowie fan." Black lipstick and a perpetual sneer? "She's definitely a punk." Spandex and a sweatband?

> "Probably lost in the eighties and doesn't know how to get out."

No one was blending in; that would have been social suicide. It was a time when style wasn't picked off a rack; it was stitched into who you were. Individuality was the name of the game, even if it meant stitching studs onto your own leather jacket or bleaching and colouring your mullet with whatever chemicals were lying around under the kitchen sink (RIP, many a bathroom wall).

Whether you were a Goth, Punk, Rocker, Mod, New Romantic or a Casual, your hair was your billboard. The punk era's Mohicans were my personal favourites when it came to styling – nothing said dedication like hair that doubled as a weapon. The amount of gel, hairspray, and sheer willpower required to maintain those vertical marvels was nothing short of heroic. They were walking art installations, navigating through doorways and carefully avoiding low ceilings. Punk attire consisted mostly of leather trousers, jackets, studded wristbands, neck collars and Dr Marten boots. Then, when the sun came out, Summer brought out their inventive side with tartan drainpipe trousers – perfect for the warmer weather. Complimented with a leather waistcoat exposing the arms, it was punk chic at its finest. The arms could be decorated in any way you desired, from hanging chain accessories to studded leather bands and a safety pin or three for good measure.

I love the artistry in this culture. It's like someone decided rebellion needed a touch of individualistic class and a whole lot of leather. The time and attention it took to put these outfits together – the payoff was nothing short of fabulous and always attracted a long gaze and close scrutiny from me.

> I was completely captivated by every chain, every spike and every defiant detail.

Despite their fierce appearance, I couldn't keep away. My fascination with their mohawk had me bursting with questions. I fully expected these guys to be all gruff and edgy, the kind of conversationalists who'd grunt more than talk. How wrong I was! It was funny how a few safety pins and a studded neck collar could mask the façade of a polite, laid-back bloke who was more than ready to dive into deep chats about anything Philosophy – or launch into his passion rant about why the government was absolute rubbish.

The girl punks wore the same anarchic uniform but with fishnets, combat boots, heavy eye makeup, and the usual trademark black lipstick. Their hair ranged from edgy and severe to "call the cops". Always bold, always unapologetically them. They were always a mystery to me.

I, on the other hand, was painfully mainstream – a plain Jane in a sea of "screw your conformity." And I knew they saw it too. You could feel the unspoken question hanging in the air. "What's she doing here?"

I didn't match. Not in clothes, attitude, or the way I styled my hair like someone who definitely didn't know the first thing about anarchy. But I stood there anyway, the bland among the iridescent rainbow, trying to figure them out, while they were probably trying to figure out why I hadn't legged it yet.

I was never going to get the opportunity to be a punk, not with my mother and my strict Catholic schooling.

The wildness of the punk outfits, and those short leather skirts didn't fit with Bernadette's ethos. Her stern motto was,

> "Sit up straight, shoulders back, and keep your legs together."

She'd add, "Skirts need to be knee-length and not too much flesh on display. You always need to leave something to the man's imagination.

Because apparently, Victorian propriety was alive and well at our school, and certainly in our home.

At thirteen, I experimented with lightening my hair with "Sun-in" spray, though "Brass-in" would be a better description. My head of house teacher decided my hair didn't look natural anymore, so instructed me to stand outside the headmaster's office every break until I returned my hair to its natural tone. I stood in exile for a week, bringing a bit of Rock 'n' roll anarchy to our buttoned-up school uniform, my friends walking past me in the corridor, giggling as I dared to rock the boat.

This fun little experiment did get me back to the place I loved though, the hairdresser's chair, Yvonne's Hair Salon, to make me look boring again. Yvonne, another local hairdressing legend. Although I loved the punk image and style, Thank God I loved rock music more, a far more relaxed uniform, and a lot less commentary from Bernadette.

It may have had its wild side, but at least it didn't require constant vigilance over the precise alignment of one's knees. And it meant I could still walk through the school gates without the teachers clocking me as a full-blown menace to society.

Music taste was crucial and dictated which personal style you were going to develop. In a way, music chose you, not the other way around.

And the records – vinyl was our sacred artefact. If a song came on the radio that made your heart thump, you'd be out the door before the DJ could finish his sentence, legging it to the record shop to ensure you bagged a copy. Getting the album home and peeling off the plastic? Pure ecstasy. Some of those covers were proper works of art; you'd sit there cross-legged, soaking up the atmosphere and smelling the newness of the sleeve for some reason. Then you'd slip the record out, careful not to smudge it, and lower the needle down. The crackle. The hiss. Those were part of the magic, weren't they? And if it came with the lyrics inside? Well, you'd lock yourself away for days, reading every word, learning every obscure B-side, every bridge, every weird instrumental interlude, until you knew the album better than your own parents.

Then came the cassettes. Sure, you could throw those in the car, which felt like pure freedom, belting out the tunes while you burned down the road, but they didn't hold a candle to the ritual of vinyl. You'd rewind and fast-forward like a maniac, hoping you'd land close to your song, like some high stakes guessing game. Still, you couldn't deny the thrill of making a mixtape, though there was an art to making the perfect one; you'd spend hours arranging the songs in the perfect order, and one slip of the fast forward could undo your investment.

Still, there's something deeply romantic about giving someone a tape full of songs you thought said, "I like you." Or

> "I'm weirdly obsessed, and here's a four-hour compilation to prove it."

Then, bam! – CDs came along. No rewinding, no flipping, just a slick shiny disc you could slip into anything with a slot. It was modern, it was convenient. CDs were the scrubbed-up polite cousin who never did anything wrong. It was like the music got cleaned up too much, lost that bit of grit, that personal touch.

But like an old friend who never left, vinyl hung in the background. And now it's come roaring back because nothing beats flipping through a stack of albums and finding a hidden gem. Streaming playlists can't hold a candle to dropping that needle and hearing that first, glorious crackle. It's pure nostalgia and a beautiful waste of time, and we wouldn't have it any other way. In my formative years, my bedroom was a shrine to the New Romantics – Duran Duran, Spandau Ballet, ABC and Japan, the lot of them pouting down at me with their frilly shirts and smudged eyeliner. But, as music evolved, I soon traded the moody glam for the gritty edge of rock. One by one, the pretty boys in ruffled collars came down off my walls, replaced by shaggy hair, denim and leather.

Back in the 80s, being a rock chick meant you wore your loyalties quite literally on your sleeve.

> My go-to outfit as a teen? A denim jacket, so heavy with band patches, it could've doubled as a bulletproof vest.

The hard rock band, Rainbow blazed across the shoulder, bold and unapologetic with Black Sabbath tucked underneath for good measure. Deep Purple and Motörhead were slapped down the sleeves, so no one could mistake me for anything less than a full-blown rock devotee.

I was addicted to the excitement of a talented rock band tearing up the stage, with legendary guitar riffs and solos, and a rhythm section that had your head banging to the beat. Their energy and expression made my heart beat faster.

I would always describe my music tastes as eclectic.

From Johnny Rotten to Maria Callas, and there's always room for a bit more. My ears dictated what I liked and enjoyed. Beyond the delights of a well-muted power cord, U2, with the imploring resonance of Bono's voice and the unique guitar style of the Edge, this band caught my attention and has held it ever since.

Ah, the mid-80s – the era when English football fans, once content with a pint and a pie, suddenly became style icons. I'm not talking Saville row fashion here, more like Saville gone rogue. The nouveau riche of the terraces, swaggering around in their newly acquired "European" fashion. And I say "acquired" with the loosest possible definition of the term.

One moment, these lads were scraping the bus fare to a stadium, the next, they're strutting around in Segio Tacchini like they've closed a deal in Monaco. Where did these brands come from? And more importantly, how on earth could they afford it? Turns out, they couldn't – at least not in the conventional sense.

English football supporters in the late 70's, early 80's, were travelling by ferry and train to European matches.

Casual culture and its obsession with designer brands began in the late 70's and grew slowly through football terrace interactions and was taken up by the hardcore hooligans as a tribal identity.

Now, I'm sure they planned to soak in the culture, maybe pick up a little wine and cheese – but apparently, the only thing they were really keen on "picking up" was an assortment of European sportswear'

Picture it: Milan 1985. A group of lads, fresh off their travel pilgrimage, walk into a shop. Now, if you've ever seen British football fans abroad, you'll know they are as subtle as a bull in a China shop. But this was no ordinary shopping spree. This was a coordinated performance.

- STEP 1: Create a bit of noise – perhaps loudly asking if this Kappa jumper comes in "football hooligan size".

- STEP 2: While the assistant is trying to comprehend what is going on, a swift hand "acquires" the item in question.
- Step 3: Exit like a greyhound with your loot, pursued by confusion.

And just like that, they returned home, brandishing their loot like gladiators, fresh from battle, only now dressed head to toe in Lacoste. A five-fingered discount, no less. By the time they were back at the pub, they were suddenly "men of taste", sipping lager, heads held high, convinced they'd just returned from a fashion pilgrimage. And we, the bystanders, wondered how they were still rocking the knockoff "Adidas trackie."

Meanwhile back in the home of denim....

I loved everything from Whitesnake to Motorhead. The melodic sounds, the pitch, the range of the lead singers – I revelled in their talent and the power ballads and anthems they created. The long shaggy hair of these demi-gods got my attention. I adored their earthiness and free spirit, and the way they mixed denim and leather for maximum effect. They seemed very real, not staged in any way, just a bunch of cool characters. They had this magical ability to hypnotise an entire stadium into a synchronised sea of air guitars. I was hooked.

Over the years, I've seen countless live bands, and being a huge U2 and Queen fan, I've had some unforgettable experiences. You know the kind of bands that don't just perform but create a spectacle? That's what these guys were. No pretentiousness, just pure, unadulterated Rock 'n' roll.

I was one of the lucky few who managed to snag a ticket to a certain event in the Summer of 1985. This was the pinnacle in my concert-going career.

> Live Aid was one of those events that feels more like a fever dream than a memory,

but for anyone who watched it on TV, it still holds a special place in the social consciousness. Billed as the "Global Jukebox", tickets were like gold dust, with the lucky few cramming into two stadiums – Wembley in London and JFK Stadium in Philadelphia.

During the latter part of 1984, nightly television news reports showed in harrowing detail just how acute and desperate the plight of the people of Ethiopia was.

The kind of images you couldn't shake, of children starving to death in front of your eyes.

People were starving, suffering and dying in horrific numbers as a terrible consequence of seemingly endless drought conditions in that area at that time.

Bob Geldof, the lead singer of the Boomtown Rats, was fuelled by outrage at the apparent inability of those in power to deliver desperately needed aid. Determined to take action, he teamed up with Midge Ure, lead singer of the band, Ultravox - and a fellow figure in the pop industry. Together they devised a plan that they hoped would bring relief to help the Ethiopian people. In their time of need.

Along with many others, they created 'Band Aid' – featuring the talents of many of the top stars in the UK pop music scene at the time.

First, they recorded and launched the Band Aid single "Do They Know It's Christmas?

The UK rallied wholeheartedly behind the Band Aid initiative, queuing up throughout December and long into 1985, to purchase the single – with its powerful plea to "Feed the World". Buying the record became a collective act of compassion, a way for everyone to feel they were contributing to what seemed like the cause of the century.

It instantly became a smash hit, skyrocketing to number one with record-breaking success.

It became the fastest-selling single in UK history at that time, shifting a million copies in its first week alone. Within a year of its release, it had raised an astonishing £8 million for the Band Aid Charitable Trust. But the single alone wouldn't be enough to provide efficient enough relief to solve the problem which was getting increasingly worse.

Something of a much greater magnitude was needed. Something as yet never created or experienced in the annals of human civilization.

It required something... Historic.

9

LIVE AID

DO THEY KNOW IT'S CHRISTMAS

LIVE AID?

That was another level entirely. The greatest show on earth; nothing had been done on this scale before. Not a penny was paid to any artist in the line-up, and no managers or PRs telling artists what they can and can't do. They just showed up, giving it everything they had and then some. It was a battle of the legends, vying to outshine each other.

> I remember the sheer giddy excitement of clutching my ticket,

and the bustling journey from Barnsley down to Wembley in a white Sherpa van was an adventure in itself. The sherpa was packed to the brim with snacks, vibrating with the excitement of five scrappy Northerners, convinced we were about to witness history, and by God, we weren't wrong. I was the youngest in the crew, which felt like a badge of honour at the time.

Once we hit London, we chucked the van on a side street, ramping it up on the curb. It was pure rock 'n' roll rebellion – abandoning our vehicle as if we'd hijacked it just for the gig. Then we legged it into Wembley, and the moment we stepped inside, you could feel this pulse, like electricity surging through 72,000 people all at once.

I headed straight to the merchandise area to buy my Live Aid T-shirt and naturally, another poster for my bedroom wall.

When we found our seats – the left-hand side, eye level to the stage and close to the front, it was like winning the lottery.

The place filled up quickly and before we knew it, Bob Geldof was escorting Princess Diana and Prince Charles to their royal seats. A quick blast of "God Save the Queen," and then, Bam!

Status Quo exploded onto the stage with "Rockin' All Over the World." ... and the crowd was in it, fully and completely. I swear, the entire stadium started bouncing like it might launch into orbit.

> Every band that hit that stage seemed to raise the bar, each one taking the crowd higher. It was like a factory reset for the soul.

Paul Young, Style Council, Dire Straits, and The Who, all out to prove that this was the gig of their lives.

And then there was that pinnacle moment when Bowie introduced The Cars video, Drive. As we watched the video on the big screens of the unimaginable suffering in Ethiopia, the whole stadium fell silent. It was like the music just stopped time. That song will always bring a lump to my throat. As we all stood, heads bowed just for that moment, it hit us how wildly lucky we were.

We were witnessing practically every music legend on the planet, all for the bargain price of twenty-five pounds – a ticket to history itself.

Meanwhile, the rest of the world was glued to their TVs, dialling in donations while Bob — bless him — stared into the cameras and demanded, "Give us your fucking money!". No one was arguing while

Bob screamed! People dug deep. It was a weird, beautiful mix of punk chaos and pure-hearted generosity, and we were right in the middle of it.

> Phil Collins really took the cake, though. The man performed at both venues on the same day!

After performing in Wembley, we watched him take off from London to Philadelphia on Concorde, broadcast live on the big screen. It was like a 'hold my beer moment" in rock history, leaving us all thinking, well if Phil can do that, maybe anything is possible. It was a wild and glorious day where music really did feel like it could save the world, and for that one moment, it probably did.

But the real show-stoppers? For me, it was U2 and Queen. Those performances were seismic, like tectonic plates shifting under Wembley. I was out of my seat, all elbows and determination, pushing through the sweaty bodies, trying to get as close to the stage as I could. Bono did what only Bono dared to do: he reached down and plucked a girl out of the crowd and gave her a full-on smooch right there on the stage. The crowd went ballistic, and she was one lucky girl having an unforgettable experience. And Freddie – well, he didn't just steal the show; he owned it, commandeering the stage like it was his own private kingdom. He was in a league of his own, practically summoning a storm with that voice of his. These performances catapulted both U2 and Queen to new heights, showcasing not just their catalogue but their raw, unmatched talent.

It was a launchpad that turned them from rock stars into legends, leaving no doubt they'd just carved their names into music history.

Every musician on stage gave it their all, but there was something about the magic of that day, seeing so many successful and long-standing artists in one go for a cause that felt bigger than any of us.

Then George Michael stepped up, his voice gliding into that unforgettable final duet with Elton John, before the stage flooded with every artist under the sun, ready to close with that iconic charity anthem that still gives us goosebumps.

It was like a collective worship – an epic musical love we all wished would never end. After ten solid hours of musical magic, we knew we'd squeezed every last note out of those bands.

It was one of the largest satellite link-ups and television broadcasts of all time, with an estimated 1.9 billion people, including 150 nations, tuning in to watch the live broadcast. As every band hit the stage for the finale, we realised we'd seen something unrepeatable. And we had.

> We walked away exhausted, elated, and completely drained, humming that anthem all the way home.

It wasn't just a concert – It was a one-of-a-kind moment in time, where music, hope, and a ragtag white van full of dreamers collided to make it to the best event ever. Every time I think about it, there's still that little kick in my heart. My Live Aid programme still holds a place of honour in my reading rack.

It was that day that ignited the fire in me. Seeing so many incredible artists in one go was like opening Pandora's box- but instead of chaos, it unleashed a lifetime of obsession. From that moment, I became a devoted disciple of live music, queuing up for every concert ticket I could get my hands on. Back then, getting tickets wasn't the smooth online operation it is now. Oh no, it was a test of endurance and camaraderie. You had to physically queue, often arriving at the crack of dawn- or practically camping out- just to secure a spot in the line.

By the time you finally clutched that sacred piece of paper, you'd often bonded with the folks around you. Come concert day, you'd meet those same people for a pint, already kindred spirits united by music. Over the years, I've witnessed moments of greatness-music that carved itself into my soul. Stevie Nicks, an ethereal powerhouse; Fleetwood Mac, with Mick Fleetwood delivering percussion like no other; Genesis, Van Halen, Def Leppard and too many more to mention, but you get the drift.

Then there was Whitney Houston, her voice a thing of unmatched beauty, and Tina Turner, a hurricane of energy and emotion.

> We even managed front-row tickets for Tina, and my mum had the pleasure of handing her a rose like an offering to royalty.

Tina, radiant as ever, descended the stairs with her electric presence, microphone in hand, belting out Nutbush City Limits. And then, as if anointing us with stardom, she leaned in, inviting us to join the chorus. Yes, I sang Nutbush with Tina Turner, even if it was for one blissful second.

Some artists were singers, others were performers, but the rare few who could do both captured hearts like no other. Neil Peart of Rush gave a masterclass in drumming precision, while George Michael on his comeback tour was unforgettable- a seamless blend of charisma and raw talent. At one point, I even fancied myself as "Liz Buble," utterly captivated by Michael Buble's romantic warbling talent and slick style.

But my heart belongs to U2. I've seen them five times, and each performance left its mark on me. From their early days to their ever-evolving sound, they've been a constant presence. Anchoring my memories with every song. Bono's voice, the Edge's guitar, the pulse of Larry and Adam's rhythm section- it all resonates deeply, as though their music has taken permanent residence in my soul.

And lastly, let's talk about the Queen herself.

> Stevie Nicks has cast her spell over generations with her gossamer bell sleeves, shawls, and mystic persona.

She's not just a singer or a songwriter; she's a storyteller, weaving tales of love, heartbreak, resilience and magic with every note and lyric.

Her presence on stage feels otherworldly like she's stepped out of a dream to remind you that strength can exist in vulnerability and femininity is a power all on its own.

Those flowing bell sleeves- part of her iconic bohemian style- are more than just fashion. They're symbols of freedom and expression, the physical manifestation of a spirit unwilling to be tethered. She has shown that you can be fierce, soft, commanding, and tender all at once.

Her music and presence are a reminder that authenticity shines brighter than conformity.

Having seen her in concert, I've witnessed this transformative energy first-hand.

Her voice, a raspy, spellbinding wail, carries the weight of experience and emotion. Every flick of her wrist, every spin in those layered chiffon skirts, feels like a call to embrace your own individuality unapologetically.

She invites you into her world, where it's okay to feel deeply, dream wildly, and be wholly yourself.

She's a reminder to lead with passion, wear your unique style proudly, and trust in the magic of your journey, whether it's through hairdressing, storytelling, or life itself.

Live music isn't just sound- it's an experience, a connection, and a memory that lingers forever. For me, it's been the soundtrack to pure moments of magic.

BUT BACK TO being fifteen years old.

10

9 TO 5

DOLLY PARTON

FRESH OUT OF HIGH SCHOOL, in the Summer of 84, I boarded a train to Skegness, a bustling seaside resort on England's East coast. At fifteen, I donned my waitressing uniform at the Ocean café, working full-time for a Greek family who ran the place. It was a busy café restaurant selling fish and chips and groundbreaking authentic doner kebabs. A new taste sensation in its day, made with love and by the hand of the father which had the locals queuing down the street.

Knee-deep in customer service and social interaction, I was part of a super-efficient crew, learning the ropes and loving every minute. I lived on site above the cafe, my first experience of being away from home and my first real taste of the working world. Boy did it get me on my feet.

Especially taking meals for the grandad of the family who lived up a steep never-ending staircase at the top of the building with a sea view and seagulls for friends. Being a man of few words, a grateful nod from the Greek man was the general exchange for the food and tea tray services.

The family took to me like one of their own in this sweet period. Eight weeks later, they gifted me with a beautiful gold necklace as I turned sixteen. After my stint there was done, I departed with enough stamina to wield a heavy turbo hair dryer.

I had been quite spoiled at the café. The wages were very good for a fifteen-year-old considering they had provided a roof over my head and meals were included. Of course, my future earnings would be half as much, euphemistically called a "training allowance" to mask the fact that we would be working long hours on our feet from dawn till dusk.

It was early September and with my first real salary cautiously saved from the seaside restaurant, I decided to treat myself. So, I took a trip to Rackhams' department store in Sheffield to buy myself a sheepskin coat and gloves. After all, winter was around the corner, and I would soon be spending quality time at bus stops. I chose a luxurious grey tone that was the latest in fashion, complementing my blonde hair perfectly. I felt quite pleased with my lavish yet practical purchase, convinced I was the epitome of style and sensibility.

I had already been accepted onto a Youth training scheme in hairdressing, the go-to route for many trades in the 80s.

After an induction week in the training school, my first placement took me to a small hair salon frequented by the blue rinse brigade. The blue hue was the ultimate statement: not quite lavender, not quite silver, but a shade that whispered, I've seen some things, and I'm still fabulous. They would march into the salon with an air of authority, handbags at the ready, and leave with their crown of carefully lacquered waves. This is where I learned the basics from a fabulous team of ladies who could set hair in their sleep.

The salon owner, Julie, was a true innovator known for manipulating hair into any masterpiece imaginable. This was evident in the heaving appointment book and a queue of ladies sitting in rows underneath the overhead dryers, hairnets fixed securely, with the distinct aroma of setting lotion permeating the air.

Each lady emerged from the combing out chair with her own Hollywood starlet aura – the romantic waves of Rita Hayworth to Audrey Hepburn's neat French roll. Some had spent years committed to a full head bleach and toning ritual, all in the quest to achieve that perfect platinum blonde bombshell look, just like Marylin Monroe. Their dedication was especially impressive.

Here's a fun fact: bleached hair is like a sponge, ready to soak up whatever the atmosphere throws at it. Back in the day of pubs, clubs and chain-smoking bingo halls, nicotine tainted every surface, it was inescapable. The result? That crisp icy blonde you left the salon with would morph into a questionable yellow hue faster than you can shout "house!" – a sort of airbrushed yellow cast brought to you by Benson & Hedges. It didn't matter how much toner you slapped on; if you spent your Saturday nights in a smoke-filled working men's club, your hair was basically auditioning to be a nicotine patch. Forget 'sun-kissed – this was 'smoke-kissed' – and there wasn't a shade chart for that.

Perms were all the rage back then. Thanks to their popularity,

> every hairdresser's salon had that unmistakable smell of perm solution that knocked you over as you walked through the door,

potent enough to make you go nose blind after five minutes – the modern day equivalent would be a trip to, Lush, but swap out that comforting waft of vanilla and lavender for a full-on nasal assault of chemicals so strong, you'd be tasting it by lunchtime.

As a salon of traditional techniques, we had our charming quirks, but I liked to spice things up by bringing in new ideas from training school. Especially in cutting techniques. We were learning from each other, blending old-school charm with modern flair which felt like a win for everyone. Anyone who has been in the hairdressing game long enough will tell you – "You never stop learning!"

My mannequin doll, Violet, was my partner in crime in the early days, my slightly creepy ally in my quest to master the art of hair. She was slightly less chatty than the average client but indispensable to my learning. Violet was my patient model for everything, and always available when I needed her. Colouring, braiding, blow drying, and the odd trim, without so much as a flinch. Lucky for me, I had a boss like

Julie, who saw my enthusiasm and decided I might be capable of handling a real human head. She started me off with basic trims and blow drys, and to my surprise, no one ran screaming from the chair. Each small success increased my confidence and helped me get ahead of the game.

It was at this salon, I learned how uniqueness in your skills would set you apart. I also learned the golden rule of greeting ladies of a certain age. Never, under any circumstances, ask, "How are you?" This question alone would set off a catalytic event, with each and every lady enthusiastic to chat, and on mass. They would overshare every tragic event, illness and medication plan they were enduring. A competition would arise of who had nearly died, who should have died and who was lucky to be alive.

Suddenly, I found myself learning more about ailments and pharmaceuticals than I ever cared to know.

> As a young hairdresser new to the scene, I quickly understood that diplomacy and carefully selected language would also be needed in my skill set.

HAIR TRAFFIC CONTROL

By the end of my stint there, I would nod sympathetically and artfully steer the subject back to the weather whilst clicking the kettle on to make them a nice cuppa.

The salon was small and quaint, with no bathroom facilities, but we had an arrangement with a neighbouring convenience store. It involved using their outside loo, a friendly set-up where we'd ask for the key in-store and return it afterward.

One day, I trotted across the street for a quick pee. I grabbed the key, as usual, and sat on the toilet, as usual.

Mid-flow, I felt the toilet suddenly dislodge as it gave way beneath me and broke in half.

In a state of shock, I managed to balance myself without falling over, while water trickled and began to tidal wave around my ankles.

Grabbing the toilet roll holder, my first thought was, "How on earth am I going to explain this? I've somehow managed to break a solid porcelain toilet." Why did this have to happen on my visit?

I walked into the shop, taking deep breaths and feeling somewhat embarrassed. Thankfully, a customer was at the end of a chat and just leaving.

As I handed over the key, I explained what had happened to the lady owner, whose look of amazement was priceless. She shook her head in confusion, eyeing my size 10 frame, clearly thinking she had misheard me. I repeated, "Sorry, but the toilet just fell in half" shrugging my shoulders as to what more intricate detail I could offer about my toileting habits.

She was surprisingly okay about it, probably because there wasn't a fitting response to such a situation.

Walking back into the salon and announcing that we don't have a toilet for the immediate future isn't exactly the news I wanted to deliver. Especially when one of the stylists is pregnant and eyeing me like I'm a ticking time bomb.

As a junior, I was already at the bottom of the pecking order. Trashing the only toilet on offer rewarded me with a collection of blank, confused stares. I stood there, sheepishly waiting for the inevitable questions. They never came. Instead, everyone seemed to silently process the fact that their bathroom breaks now involved a trek to "who-knows-where?" I could almost hear them thinking, "How did she manage to break a toilet?"

Finally, the pregnant stylist sighed,

> "Well, I guess it's time to get creative."

And just like that, I solidified my reputation as the junior who managed to take down a porcelain throne.

My friend Ann has never let me forget that mortifying incident. When I told her, she laughed so hard she couldn't breathe. That's her speciality – laughing at every absurd thing that happens to me and finding every disaster hilariously entertaining.

With much affection and a great start with Julie, I moved on to a larger family salon – with its own toilet.

The buzz of the Health & Hair studio was electric, a central hub in the same small town, complete with a gym, sauna, beauty room and solarium. It was a temple where hair met health and vanity had its own postcode.

11

BUFFALO STANCE
NENEH CHERRY

THE 80S WERE in full swing. Big hair and even bigger egos strutted their stuff and aerobics was the latest craze. Every class was packed, full of women bouncing in neon leotards and leg warmers, looking like they had just stumbled out of Olivia Newton-John's, *Physical* video.

It was somewhere in the late 80s during an aerobics class where I was furiously trying to keep up, that I first spotted the now-infamous lower-back tattoo, staring back at me from a young woman in the row ahead. At this time, this was edgy stuff. The Inky art would generally be a pretty small butterfly or flower - tasteful but suggestive, hinting at rebellion just out of sight.

This soon became the latest, 'must-have', fashion statement, a little ink secret for those brave enough to join the tattoo wave. With hipster leggings and crop tops in vogue, these " tramp stamps" were on full display, flashing like a secret signal every time someone touched their toes. The 80s had unlocked a new chapter of decorative body art, ready for the 90s

The hairstyles were just as diverse and demanding – short pixie crops, tramlines, vibrant colours with bleached tips.

> Offset Bobs with choppy fringes and infamous long spiral perms were all the rage.

Over time, I accumulated skills in all areas, working in the gym and collecting a few beautician skills. I was a hair model magnet, accelerating to the equivalent of a 3rd-year stylist in twelve months.

Not the usual time scale but I was driven, securing myself a hairdressing apprenticeship when they were becoming scarce. I would chase down ladies on their way to the shops and ensnare them with a sweet smile and the offer of a cuppa. They were happy to oblige and soon became regulars knowing a senior stylist would oversee my work. The intense training paid off when I won a hair colouring competition at day release college, landing me in a local newspaper feature and a boost in clientele.

Ann was my hair model for this competition, and it felt like a win for both of us given our childhood history. We were visited by a few photographers who were keen to get shots of me re-creating the winning image. She looked super glamorous with an edgy razor cut complimented with a cherry black base, bright copper top and bleach blonde hair tips combo which got us through to the regional finals. I didn't win any trophies there, but hey, for a seventeen-year-old, just getting that far was a big deal.

THE 80S WERE a wild playground of inventive styles and outrageous fashion. No two people dared to look the same. What truly lit my fire, though, was the yearly local hair competitions. Each stylist brought jaw-dropping flair and talent, miles beyond your everyday salon requests. But the *Fantasy* section? That was the crown jewel. It was pure, unfiltered creativity – the kind that made me fall head over heels for my craft all over again.

Back then, we didn't have today's endless rainbow of colouring options, fancy styling products or high-tech tools for curling and smoothing.

> It was all about tongs and hot rollers, especially when it came to wedding hair.

Curling wands? Straighteners? Dream on.

Blow drying was a full-body workout requiring brute force, and a hairdryer with the heat of a small furnace to get that hair cuticle flat and shiny.

We couldn't keep up with the demand for long spiral and corkscrew perms. It was like a perm factory with every winding technique.

To finish, the diffuser dryer volumizing the curls was an experience. Picture women's heads dangling upside down in their chairs, less salon and more a Cirque du Soleil while gravity worked its magic. Fridays were prime blow-dry days, a symphony of whirring dryers and the chatter of clients spilling their weekend plans. It was practically a weekly ritual, getting their hair polished and on point for whatever glamorous adventures lay ahead.

Not every hairstyle and colour was a triumph, though, but it's through our mishaps that we master colour corrections and refine our judgement. Experience teaches us to say no to certain requests like the time a regular client asked me about colouring her daughter's ginger curls with crazy bright red highlights. I explained the whole ordeal: the pre-lightening with bleach, the inevitable fading of the red pigment with each wash, and how I didn't think the colours would complement each other.

But the teenage daughter pleaded with her mother so persistently that finally, I caved in, confident that I had covered all the bases on the advice and upkeep of this drastic change.

And so, the daughter arrived at her appointment, happily seated in my colour trophy winner's chair, and soon enough, she emerged with a mass of luminous red curls atop her ginger locks. She was thrilled, shaking her vibrant new mane as she waltzed out of the salon into the world outside.

Meanwhile, my heart sank. I felt like I had made a pact with the devil. People would inevitably ask who was responsible for this unique blend, and my name was now tied to this Ronald McDonald-inspired transformation.

Sharing the story with fellow stylists, they burst into fits of laughter, reassuring me that it would all be fine. They joked she was probably out there enjoying a year's supply of free chicken nuggets and Mcflurrys.

Big lesson learned. I will again say, we learn more from our failures than our successes. And sometimes, those failures are just too colourful to forget.

As with all small communities, the gym and hair studio brimmed with a delightful assortment of characters. In any gym, you will always find those special few who fancy themselves as the object of universal desire, strutting about just to catch a mere glimpse of themselves, flexing in every reflective surface they pass.

> In our gym the general name for him was Bob. And Bob was 'a gift to all women'.

We had a veritable parade of Bobs. And when I say parade, I mean a slow procession of awkwardness, each Bob with his own distinct flair for making you reconsider every life choice that led you to this point.

First, there was Boring Bob, with his endless droning on tales of mundane trivia inspiring early yawns from everyone. His trivia was less, "fun facts" and more "why am I here?" You'd nod along but your mind was drifting to what was for dinner that night.

Then there was Creepy Bob, who had mastered the art of making even a treadmill feel uncomfortable. He lingered just a bit too long, staring a bit too intently, and you'd find yourself suddenly needing to be anywhere else. The treadmills practically sighed with relief when he left.

Now Carpets Under the Arms Bob introduced us to body hair as a winter coat. Sidling up to the front desk, leaning in close, his breath a curious mix of coffee and desperation only to ask if there were any "special" treatments on offer. It took all my willpower not to offer a restraining order instead or an urgent gift card for waxing.

Now, let's not forget Ginger Bob, harmless enough, you might think, with his green freckles to boot, but lacking Mick Hucknall vibes. His bright hair served as a beacon, warning all to keep a safe distance.

 And finally, Gobby Bob.

This one had the confidence of someone who'd downed six espressos and had ten conversations running simultaneously. As soon as he opened his mouth, your brain went into panic mode, and your ears folded in self-defence. He'd chatter away so fast your synapses would scramble, trying to keep up.

Of course, politeness was part of the job, but dealing with Bobs required an extra layer of diplomacy. Overzealous Bobs demanded an intricate dance of cordial nods and strategically timed bathroom breaks avoiding any conversational booby traps. "Sorry, I've got a client waiting," was my usual deflection. Navigating the sea of Bobs was a workout itself, the key was to sidestep and smile, always keeping one eye on the nearest exit.

One evening, after a long shift at the studio I had locked up and was waiting for the bus home, visions of tea and toast in my head, when suddenly —- screech! —-

Creepy Bob, pulled up beside me, now rebranded as Curb-Crawling Bob. He rolled down the window with the swagger of a man who thought his, Vauxhall Nova was a babe magnet of Aston Martin DB5 proportions. His veiny arm gripping the door window frame tightly, so he could flex his bicep and show off his tan.

"Need a lift anywhere?" he said, flashing a grin that would have made Jack Nicholson nervous. His timing was suspiciously perfect, considering the gym closed at the same time each evening.

Where was Bus Driver Bob when I needed him?

"Oh no, thanks, I'm waiting for the last bus", I said, hoping Police Bobby, Bob might be making his rounds in the very near vicinity.

Outside of work, the last thing anyone needs is a dubious member of the Bob community, creeping up into your peripheral vision.

Overall, I considered myself particularly fortunate to work in this environment which seemed to magnetise successful competition bodybuilders from near and far. The gym was a mixed bag with women's and men's nights, but the locals? They were in heaven, training alongside of these muscle-bound marvels. It wasn't just about lifting weights, it was about tapping into their endless fitness wisdom as if by proximity, they might somehow all end up with abs like theirs.

Occasionally, we would host Body-building Seminars where the tickets would sell out faster than you could say "flex". These events featured posing demonstrations, nutrition tutorials and fitness and training schedules, finishing with a Q&A session with the audience.

One seminar sticks in my mind. A rather earnest bodybuilder passionately promoting the importance of mixing protein and carbs in your diet. As he waxed lyrical about macronutrients, a young guy in the audience innocently raised his hand and asked, "Does that mean I can have chips and egg?" The room erupted into laughter, followed by a spontaneous round of applause. The bodybuilder caught off guard, managed to crack a smile and say, "Well, not quite where I was going, but dip your bread in while you're at it!"

Those were the days when bodybuilding advice was gospel and fitness enthusiasts revelled in mingling with the pros.

In the run-up to a bodybuilding competition, the place was like a boot camp. The competitors would be prowling around in full beast mode, dead-focused on psyching themselves up with the intensity of warriors going into battle. That was our cue to steer clear.

They were in "the zone" – all-day training sessions, breaking only to devour an entire roast chicken like it was a perfectly reasonable snack.

My one sacred duty? To get them stage-ready, slathering them in enough fake tan to make a mahogany table jealous and then step back to check

if it was even with the right tone of deep bronze......
well orange.

After the last swipe, I'd give them a pat on the shoulder (if I dared) and wish them well, knowing full well they wouldn't remember a word of it. They were already visualising victory on the podium - and that post-competition pizza.

> The Health & Hair Studio was a temple of 80s hedonism and a great place to solidify my training.

Sure we were serious about fabulous hair and toned bodies and beyond that, the beauty area was buzzing with waxing and facials, and tanning beds that turned people into walking toffee apples. The place screamed *lifestyle*.

The large sauna churned out a eucalyptus aroma like it was trying to fumigate the entire street, and the place always carried a heady mix of hairspray, sweat, and ambition. Clients popped in for a quick trim and left with an overcooked tan, a bit of scandalous gossip, and a faint smell of eucalyptus clinging to their leotards. Everyone loved it, and honestly, so did I.

Three years flew by, and just like that, my apprenticeship was over. It was time to move on and move up. A big shiny step into that glamorous world of being self-employed, well actually, with more sweeping, but slightly better tips.

12

SHE WORKS HARD FOR THE MONEY
DONNA SUMMER

AT NINETEEN, with a mishmash of skills and a set of circumstances that made me question my status, I decided to strike out on my own and upgrade my position. Learning to drive was the game-changer which had me cruising around with my scissors. Suddenly, I wasn't tied to a salon. Mobile hairdressing had potential – cosy home visits, screaming kids in highchairs, and the occasional client still in their dressing gown. I figured, why not? I could still navigate my craft in a cramped kitchen with my hairdryer in one hand, and a tea and a biscuit in the other.

> Take the leap, bite the bullet, and trust the journey. All those cliches fitted

perfectly as I plunged headfirst into the deep end of starting my own business.

Armed with sheer willpower, my scissors, and my parents cheering me on from the sidelines. I figured I might just have enough gusto to make it in the hairdressing world.

Mind you, my mother's support came with a healthy dose of selective amnesia. She conveniently overlooked the time she had to wear a headscarf for the best part of two weeks like she was auditioning for a 1970s spy film.

And yet again, she conveniently forgot why she wore that scarf – it was thanks to yours truly. Thick hair demands a battle plan. You don't just hack away and hope it behaves; you strategize like you're preparing for an invasion. That hair needs to lay right, look stylish, and still have some kind of shape four weeks later when it's gearing up for another cut.

In those early days, as I had just turned fifteen, I thought I had cracked the code. In a burst of teenage confidence, I volunteered to give Mum a "light trim."

> My approach was simple: if it stuck out, I cut it off.

Twenty minutes later, she emerged looking like Rosy from the movie Ryan's Daughter. If the brief was to create a look that screamed "windswept Irish coast." I certainly nailed it.

But still, she cheered me on.

I took my sweet time building clientele in the very area I trained.

Meanwhile, I was traipsing around the area paying for valuations of real estate, a glorified game with real consequences. I was trying to find the perfect location for my dream salon. Armed with wide-eyed optimism and zero clue about commercial property, I scouted the local high streets that ticked boxes: ample customer footfall, parking that didn't require a Sherpa to reach, and a vague whiff of potential. Each time, it was the same story. The buildings had some structural, damp proof, or leasing issue.

In the end, desperation led me to Yvonne's salon. Yvonne – local legend, hair wizard, and the woman who had rescued my hair from my teenage DIY Brass-in massacre – This was my last shot.

I waltzed in, all of nineteen and brimming with a heady mix of naivety and ambition, and just enough cheek to make it interesting, "Yvonne, would you be interested in selling your salon?"

Yvonne's expression was somewhere between startled and stifling a laugh.

Yvonne had built her salon from the ground up. It was her empire, her baby. And there I was, this bright-eyed upstart, casually proposing she hands me the keys to her kingdom.

"Sell my salon? No, I'm alright here for a while. But good on you for asking. Good luck." Her tone was kind, even encouraging.

Looking back, it wasn't a rejection. It was inspiration wrapped up in a polite "not today", and it stuck with me. Because once the right opportunity came up, all systems were go.

Yvonne might not have handed me her empire, but she did something better – she lit the fire under me to keep going with my determination to build my own.

Sure, I had to make sacrifices, like downgrading my beloved car to a basic model, all to fund the down payment for the dream of owning a salon. But it felt right, stepping back to eventually rocket forward. Hair power over horsepower, right? And within two years, bam!! I found myself in a partnership in the perfect venue. The salon needed a full fit-out and a design overhaul from scratch. A month of living in a fog of plaster, dust, paint fumes, and the relentless soundtrack of hammers and drills, every brushstroke felt like a small victory. When we finally threw open the freshly painted doors, our steady stream of loyal customers rolled up to support us – partly out of love and partly because they couldn't face another DIY fringe trim.

On the eve of the grand opening, in swept Bernadette, with a set of Paragon cups and saucers, because in her eyes, a proper cup of tea was the backbone of British civilization. No way was anyone getting a mug in this salon. If they were going to chat while I worked away my magic, they'd be doing it with proper porcelain in hand. That was Mum's touch, her way of saying, "This place is special."

The mid-90s were a quirky blend of the 80s and the emerging sleekness of the new decade. Big hair was finally bowing out, making room for those straight, stylish cuts that were suddenly everywhere. Enter the "Rachel cut", popularised by Jennifer Aniston's character in the hit US comedy series, Friends. A style you could pull off with a strong blow dry and a stash of Velcro rollers. But let's be real: The Rachel wasn't a magic ticket to looking like Jennifer Aniston. We could never promise that. You needed those cheekbones to make it sing. Velcro rollers can work wonders, but they can't rewrite your genetic code.

As we stepped into this new era, the salon took off – not with flashy ads or social media campaigns, but through pure, unfiltered word of mouth. That was real advertising and always will be. Back then, 'marketing' meant maybe splashing an offer in the local newspaper or propping an A-frame board outside the shop with a bit of your own advertising flair.

> No frills, no fuss, just a solid reputation, a lot of hard work, and standards you could guarantee to deliver on.

Clients had this fierce loyalty to their salon and stylist, and come December, that loyalty was on full display. By mid-month, the space under the Christmas tree looked like a department store – teeming with gift-wrapped goodies, boxes of chocolates, and more wine than a respectable household should see in a year. It was like some strange barter system: offer top-quality mince pies with a tipple of Sherry throughout December, and this would guarantee you enough Christmas loot to keep the festivities going well into January.

January – the sacred fortnight of hairdressing purgatory. Those rare, blissful weeks when the phone finally stops ringing, like it owes you money, and you can actually hear yourself think – "Is this what freedom feels like?" January gives us that breather. You see, December is the apocalypse of appointments. Everyone – yes, everyone – books in for their festive spruce up as if Christmas dinner is some kind of international hair competition.

By April, you've finally got things running like clockwork again, organising the appointment book into a steady manageable rhythm – just in time for the pre-Christmas bottleneck to begin again in October. It's the madness of the job and there's no escape. Just snip, laugh, repeat.

13

CALLING OCCUPANTS OF INTERPLANETARY CRAFT

THE CARPENTERS

IT WAS A CHILLY FRIDAY NIGHT, just before Christmas, and I was blissfully deep in dreamland – probably winning an argument I'd never win in real life, arguably the stuff of fantasy.

> Salon life is a whirlwind of endless client chatter, so by the time I finally crash, my brain cooks up dream sequences so absurd that they could top the box office.

Think blockbuster material with a sprinkle of comedy and a generous dollop of surrealism.

You know the type: that random guy you drive past at the bus stop every morning, the one you've never exchanged a word with, yet he's starring in your dream, living in your house. And not just living there, he's inexplicably in charge of something, like running a llama sanctuary out of your kitchen. Llamas everywhere, eating toast and judging you. It's insane, absolutely bonkers, but oddly believable when you're fast asleep.

The radiators were working overtime as they should in December, the month when hairdressers lose all concept of time and sanity, counting the days until the Christmas break. But, just before midnight, I was rudely yanked from my slumber by a noise that wasn't festive. It wasn't sleigh bells; it was knocking on the back door. The spine-chilling knocking that made you wish you had a dog to send downstairs.

I stumbled to the window, rubbed the sleep out of my eyes, and squinted into the darkness. It wasn't Santa, and it wasn't a burglar; it was something far worse, my dad! His unmistakable Irish lilt cut through the night, "Let me in Lizbeth, let me in!"

I grabbed my dressing gown and hauled myself downstairs, fully aware that my dad showing up at midnight is never good news.

But swinging the door open to find him fully dressed – shirt, tie, jacket, shoes, socks – everything, except for trousers?

Well, that's a whole new level of concern. My first thought:

"Why on earth has he got no trousers on?"

My second thought: this better not be a Christmas tradition he's just now sharing with me.

"Dad" I managed, half annoyed and half horrified, "Where are your trousers?"

He pushed past me like a man who'd just seen a ghost and slammed down at the kitchen table and whispered conspiratorially.

> "The aliens.... the aliens have taken my trousers. Don't tell Mammy,"

rubbing his forehead in a state of panic. Ah, yes, of course, the aliens. I could feel my eyebrows nudging my hairline as I attempted to process this little nugget of information.

I sighed. "Well, naturally, I'm not going to tell Mammy – she's not coming downstairs at this hour for this." Her standard response would be, "He's your blood, not mine. Deal with it!"

But seriously – ALIENS?

I tried again, "Dad. Really. Why have you got no trousers on? Where are they?"

He looked at me with all seriousness of a man recounting a close encounter of the trouser-less kind and gestured towards the door. "I don't know," he said as if the explanation was obvious. "Out there, the aliens have taken them."

Now I'm not saying I believed him, but in my battle-weary state, I did consider scanning the skies for UFOs. But logic prevailed. This wasn't about little green men; this was about my dad, who was in the middle of some bizarre pant-less nightmare.

So, there I was, standing in the kitchen at midnight, trying to coax this half-delirious man out of his alien abduction fantasy, while simultaneously wondering if this was the new normal. Dad sat there, still rubbing his forehead like a man who had witnessed the unimaginable – his trousers taken by otherworldly beings. And me? I was figuring out how to solve this mystery and get him — and his trousers — to bed. And quickly too, before Mammy woke up, we didn't want that. So, the interrogation began, with all the finesse of a crime drama.

"Where have you been? Who were you with? Did you catch the bus? Did you walk home? Has anyone hurt you or asked you for money? Tried to take money from you?"

As if he was a hardened criminal caught red-handed, I emptied his jacket pockets, hoping for clues. Out tumbled a collection of betting slips, a pen, and a hip flask with a faint whiff of moonshine – classic Dad.

But his door keys and cash? Abducted along with his trousers.

My brain was still trying to piece together this bizarre puzzle, wondering if alien abductions now involved memory loss and trouser theft. All I had was a torch and a deepening sense that this night was about to get weirder. I started in the back garden, treading the various paths, waving my torch around like a stranded ship's captain signalling for help. By now, the neighbours were well acquainted with our family antics, but even this was pushing the limits of their tolerance. I was about to give up when I spotted a glint in the flower bed. A whiskey bottle was nestled there, like a glassy, 80-proof gnome. This wasn't so much of a clue as a confirmation: whiskey had surely been involved. Still no trousers, though.

I continued down the driveway onto the street, praying I wouldn't run into anyone. Wandering around at one in the morning, in a dressing gown and slippers, armed with a torch was not on my list of things to do.

> How would that conversation even go?

You see, people in Yorkshire are super helpful but also gloriously nosey – in a "we love you, but we'll tell everyone what you did," kind of way. "Oh, just looking for the old fellas' trousers. Nothing to see here!"

Helpful nosey stranger: What style of trousers? What colour? Are they jeans?

Me: Yes, trousers, not jeans. Definitely – not jeans.

Here's a fun fact for you: Nowhere on this earth will you find an Irishman, raised in the 1940's, ever owning a pair of jeans. Not even for a casual stroll.

No, no, jeans are a foreign concept. They would sooner mow the lawn or fix the roof in what used to be their Sunday best, now tragically downgraded to 'work trousers'.

Ask anyone with Irish ancestry, I dare you. You will not find a single soul who's ever seen their dad or grandad, donning the denim.

There's more chance of aliens stealing their trousers.

Which, funnily enough, brings us back to my current predicament: hunting for trousers in the dead of night, while hoping neighbours don't think I'm the one who's lost the plot. And then, like a bolt of lightning, it hit me. Sure, the missing trousers were 'in your face', but did I ever check if he still had underpants on? Surely to God, he did. And I mean, we're talking about Irish dads' underpants? They're not just underpants. They're massive, industrial strength, and capable of doubling up as makeshift tarps. You could shelter a whole village under those things if the rain came down hard enough or set up a circus big top if the mood took you.

My stomach dropped like a stone. I hadn't checked. My mind started spiralling. What else had happened that night?

Worse yet, the thought crossed my mind – had my dad become a flasher? Please God, no.

Life was hard enough without that kind of notoriety. After a thorough search that yielded nothing but cold feet and a growing dread, I had to admit defeat. No trousers.

Returning to the house, I found Dad sat there, plonked down by the kitchen fire, bare-legged and bewildered. My brain was fried, my feet were frozen, and I had to work in a few hours. Running a salon at twenty-three was enough of a circus without dealing with midnight mysteries involving a pant-less parent.

Looking at him, I wondered if it was too much to hope for that maybe, just maybe, he still had underwear on. I gingerly lifted his shirt at the side praying that some modesty had remained.

Absolutely nothing. Not a stitch or whisper of fabric. Dad sat there as if this was the most natural state for a man his age on a Friday night, well, Saturday morning. My mind raced between pity and outright panic, as he looked at me with complete oblivion.

How on earth had he wandered the streets in this fashion and gone unnoticed? The man's a walking mystery. I couldn't exactly call the police to report a tipsy dad whose trousers had been snatched by aliens and expect them to launch a full-scale investigation. It was the silly season, and they were busy with real crimes. But I couldn't let it go – anxiety gnawed at me. I had to get back out there.

I was scanning the garden paths one last time on the brink of giving up hope when it hit me – the forgotten outside toilet.

Unused, obsolete, and more cobwebs than walls, this was where all things went to die. Including, apparently,

Dad's underpants and trousers. I swung open the dusty, half-hinged wonky door and there they were, laid out on the floor in a perfect figure eight, as if he'd just shrugged them off and wandered away, blissfully unconcerned.

Thank God my dad isn't a flasher! was all I could think as I picked them up and marched back inside. Like a very tired Miss Scarlett from Cluedo, I tossed them at him.

"There's your pants and trousers," I snapped. "I've been up half the night, and I've got to be up for work in a few hours."

> He looked genuinely relieved to be reunited with his trousers again and sheepishly apologised.

As I hauled myself back upstairs, I ran into my mum on the landing. She eyed me suspiciously. "What's all the noise about?"

In the briefest explanation I could manage, I muttered, "Aliens. Trousers. Whiskey. You name it. She just signed, "Oh, that man!", and shuffled back to bed, shutting the door on what was clearly not her first alien-related incident.

Back in my bed, I was trying to coax myself back to sleep. My mind was still whirring away as I struggled to switch off. Just as I felt the sweet embrace of sleep sneaking back in, my alarm went off like it was being paid by the bleep. My brain felt like it had run a 5K before I started.

The irony, of course, was not lost on me. As I shuffled, bleary-eyed past my dad's bedroom, there he was, door ajar, snoring like a contented bear in hibernation. Meanwhile, I had a full day of work ahead of me, and he was just getting started on his next round of snore-fest.

Motivated by years of unpaid emotional labour, I waltzed into the bathroom to prepare for battle. There it was, a sponge as big as a dinner plate, just sitting there, practically begging for mischief. Soaking it in ice-cold water, I quietly slipped into his room – "Right Matty," I thought, "time to rise and shine." I grabbed the mattress corner and BAM! I slammed it down like I was auditioning for Riverdance, squeezing that sponge over his unsuspecting face.

"WAKE UP MATTY!" I roared, with the satisfaction of a job well done. His eyes shot open, wide and wild, as if the Aliens were back.

"Not ALIENS this time, Dad", I said, delighting in his bewilderment. "It's just me, the one who has to work today." He didn't say a word. Smart move. He just rolled over and recoiled himself.

He knew exactly why the sponge had come for him – a wee reminder that chaos has consequences in this house, and I wasn't above dishing out a bit of morning justice.

And after a few slips of the tongue, that's not where the story ends.

I dragged myself into the salon, bleary-eyed but determined to survive the day. It was the run-up to Christmas, as I previously mentioned. I was already counting the hours to the end of this shift, balancing the madness from only a few hours ago with heaps of caffeine. I wasn't my usual chipper self, and naturally, clients noticed. They're sharp my lot, like detectives in hair foils. "How are you? "They asked, eyes boring into you with that mix of curiosity and concern. I replied, "Yeah, I'm good, really good." But in truth, it wasn't the best due to Dad's antics from the night before.

> At one point, I let out a yawn that could've swallowed a hair roller.

You alright love? one client pressed. The caffeine was now kicking in, and I was starting to reflect on the amusing aspect of it all.

Unable to resist, I sighed, Oh, just a bit tired. Was up till 2 am because my dad came home with no trousers on. That's when the salon froze. Brushes stopped mid-air, scissors paused mid-snip, and even the gossip mag on the shelf dropped to the floor in shock. Wide-eyed and open-mouthed, they zoomed in on me like a crowd waiting for the main act.

Now, everyone at the salon knew about Matty – my dad, the legend of unpredictability - and they were salivating for the latest instalment. I was up to my ears in appointments, trying to stay focused on Christmas hair. But they wouldn't let it go. "What did Matty do this time?" they asked, eyes gleaming in anticipation. My clients thrive on these stories – the crazier, the better. It's like they're indoctrinated into some weird, vicarious reality show. Their weekends would be incomplete without the latest tale of our family madness to share down the pub and over their Sunday roast. In the end, I knew resistance was futile. I had to carve out a little storytelling session during my thirty-minute lunch break at 12.30 pm.

"Right, everyone," I announced, Today's Feature Presentation: "I Thought My Dad Had Turned into

A Flasher." Please arrive early as salon chairs will be in short supply for this matinee.

Despite it being a manic Saturday in December, clients who had finished their appointments ducked back in, abandoning Christmas shopping and all common sense. Who knew a father losing his trousers would become the highlight of their week?

Forget haircuts and colours; they were here for the Matty and Bernie saga. I swear, if I charged for tickets, I'd have made enough to close the shop for a week. As the tale unfolded of Matty's midnight escapade, complete with the bewildered, trouser-less state and my frantic search, trawling the streets in my dressing gown, while trying to dodge imaginary aliens – you could hear the laughter pouring out of the door and onto the high street. Because for them, this wasn't just a haircut – this impromptu bit of theatre, with its front-row seats and real-life absurdity, that's what made their day. After all, December is Pantomime season.

As the laughter finally died down, I gave a mock bow. Thanks for watching folks. Same time next week.

14

THUNDERSTRUCK
AC/DC

AT TWENTY-FIVE YEARS OLD, I'd just moved into my first house – a charming little spot in a village, only a quick drive to my parents and the salon, with a pub only a few blocks away – Because, who wants to live in a dry village!

This new location, as luck would have it, was crucial for emergencies like this one. Arriving home from a busy day at the salon and minding my own business (as one does when peace and quiet are at a premium), the phone rang. It was Mum.

> "You better come over right away. We've got a bit of a situation."

"Oh, a situation, you say. What kind of a situation?"

"Well...... a small explosion actually."

Naturally, my brain went into overdrive, but before I could launch into my usual barrage of questions – "How, why, who, what?" Mum cut me off. "Just come now!"

So, I jumped in the car and sped over to my parents' house, weaving quickly through the traffic. As soon as I walked into the kitchen, I was greeted by a scene that was, in a word, bewildering.

There was Dad, with a neckerchief tied around his face, looking like a bandit from an old Western movie, darting around in a frenzy clutching a dustpan and sweeping brush. And Mum, well, Mum was seething.

Now, she's not one to lose her cool easily, as it goes with the nurse training. She generally keeps a calm and civil tongue in her head. But the look she shot me - Let's just say, her eyes were in assassin mode and her entire persona embodied a 'red mist'. At that moment, she was, rage incarnate.

"He's blown up - ALL - MY - BEST - FUCKING - CHINA !!"

she furiously announced, pointing an accusatory

finger at Dad - like a sheriff from an old Western movie, aiming to shoot a bandit.

"Look at him, running around like a bloody terrorist! And now he thinks he can stick it all back together!"

As it turned out, Dad's little DIY project with the gas poker had backfired. A gas leak had been quietly accumulating in the cupboard next to the fire, and when Dad went to light it— BOOM!!. My mum's best crockery, wine glasses, dining sets, the whole nine yards, were now part of a porcelain and glass mosaic all over the kitchen floor. There was Dad, frantically collecting shards in a bucket, trying to reassemble the mess like a deranged jigsaw puzzle master. My sister was lurking in the background, throwing nervous glances between Mum and Dad, wisely keeping her distance from the epicentre of the disaster. Dad, on the other hand, was in full-blown panic mode.

He knew he had upset Bernadette, yet again, and in his chaotic frenzy, all he could do was shout, in an increasingly high-pitched Irish warble – "All these bitching nurses in the house, and no one will help me!"

The only thing more explosive than the situation was the dramatic tone of his meltdown.

His face was beet-red, minus the eyebrows, which had been singed clean off in the small-scale detonation. He was staggering around like a shell-shocked WWI soldier, freshly blasted out of his trench, zigzagging in a blind panic, trying to dodge invisible shrapnel. Meanwhile, Bernadette loomed, like a vengeful artillery unit, locked and loaded, ready to unleash the next devastating round upon him.

So, there I was playing the role of peacemaker. I tried to calm Mum down while gently suggesting to Dad that he put down the bucket and maybe, just maybe, step away from the crime scene. After the initial shock had worn off, I decided to leave them to it and went back to my house, thinking the worst was over.

The next day, I went back to survey the aftermath. To my astonishment, Dad had somehow managed to make things worse. Before I left, I had advised him to use a cool compress and apply some Sudocrem medicated cream onto his face, which had taken quite a beating. But bless him; he'd grabbed the wrong tube and slathered on Ralgex instead – a deep heat formula. Now, his forehead and cheeks were sporting a fresh set of blisters because, apparently, one disaster wasn't enough for him.

Sometimes, no matter how hard you try, a bit of damage control just isn't enough to salvage the situation. However, the gas poker was retired, locked away to prevent any further "improvements" from Dad. And many years later, when Mum sold the house, the estate agent advised that the heating system would be condemned, an appropriately fitting and backhanded tribute to Dad's DIY escapades.

15

CAKE BY THE OCEAN
DNCE

BY THIS STAGE of the game, I'd made the grand escape from salon life and was thriving as a mobile hairdresser, which, despite the manic schedule, was surprisingly lucrative. Sure, I was ruled by the clock, with the constant feeling I was two minutes behind wherever I was supposed to be. But for all the sprinting from one house to another, I had it down to a fine art. I could cut, colour, and still make it to the school gates on time.

A hot shower to start my day was followed by a coffee so strong it could probably jump-start my car. Working gear on, a spritz of perfume to pretend I've got it all together, grab a banana on the way out for some token nod to healthiness, and I'm good to go. The breeze through the car window cleared my mind and the crisp green scenery filled me with a sense of serenity. With a carload of thoughts planning the structure of my day, the girls dropped off at school, I can finally take a breath. Now it's just me and my appointment diary.

First stop today: Ted and Perdy's place, the home of a delightful couple who had spanned decades together. Well, just Ted now. Perdy had passed away three months ago. I'd been doing their hair for ten years, and as their cottage was tucked away at the end of a long bumpy lane, they appreciated the regular service I provided. They used to joke that I was their last connection to civilization. Given their advanced age, their social life had dwindled. Their old friends had popped their clogs, and their social calendar was reduced to the occasional trip to Marks and Spencer's – via taxi, naturally.

Ted was a retired history teacher, the kind who could make even the most boring historical event sound like a thriller. Perdy, on the other hand, was a no-nonsense woman who had contributed to the war effort, then spent the rest of her life raising kids and running the house with military precision. As the parents of two successful sons and the perks of Oxbridge grandchildren, a source of immense pride, life was tickety-boo. There was much to celebrate and little to complain about.

Ted's hair was nothing short of legendary – thick, white and wild, like Beethoven after a windstorm. It demanded regular taming, whilst Perdy enjoyed a carefree perm she could pop the setting rollers in herself between my visits. Ted was glued to the telly watching the cricket. Every so often, though, he'd break his concentration, and announce, "There's a hare running across the field." Naturally, I'd press my face against the window, squinting, hoping to catch a glance of this mythical hare. But, nope, nothing. Not a twitch of movement.

Ted, meanwhile, is narrating the thing's life story, as if he had binoculars for eyes. The man had the sight of a military sniper, while I was left wondering if I needed to book an eye test. They were typical of that generation. Whilst Ted parked himself in the lounge, Purdy would rule the kitchen, doing her own thing. Perming solution on and doing its magic, Perdy, ever the gracious hostess, would ply me with tea, biscuits, and a running commentary of her latest shopping escapades.

Marks and Spencer's was her battlefield, and she had no problem taking out any obstacles, be it a slow-moving pensioner or a poorly dressed mannequin. She also had the knack for spotting unfortunate-looking babies, peering from their prams, which she gleefully dubbed "aliens."

According to Purdy, their blank stares were a clear sign that the lights were on, but nobody was home.

> Of course, faced with their doting parents — naturally — she lied through her teeth.

Praising their beautiful treasures and captivating them with her boundless charisma. Perdy could charm the birds out of the trees when she wanted to, but her wicked humour, a delightful mix of honesty and mischief, was saved for me.

Together, Ted and Perdy were a riot. I always carved out extra time for them, not just because I enjoyed their company, but because they always had me in stitches, and made it clear they relished every extra second of my visit.

They chugged along harmoniously together but as with anyone pushing One hundred, time caught up with them. Ted became bedridden, his booming history teacher voice reduced to little more than a whisper as he was losing his vocal ability.

Then unexpectedly, I got the call. Perdy had suffered a massive stroke and had gone into a nursing home. Just like that, Ted was left home alone with a care package in place and a string of carers to keep him ticking over.

In all my years as a hairdresser, particularly as a mobile one, I've been right in the thick of people's lives – intimate, raw, messy moments that most folks would rather not face. Illness, vulnerability, death – it was all part of my job. Growing up in an Irish Catholic family, funerals were a regular event.

Add to that my booming clientele of people I know over the years – some departed – my friends humorously dub me the "Grim Reaper." This title was earned, thanks to my unwavering dedication to funeral attendance plus my trusty long black coat that saw more winter grave sides than Christmas markets.

I've been to so many funerals, over a hundred and fifty and counting. I've had to set up a "death box" just to house all the memorial cards and orders of service booklets. It's like a morbid filing cabinet, stacked to the brim with tributes from over the years.

Funerals. Some people avoid them like an invite to a pyramid scheme meeting—only showing up if it's blood relative level compulsory. Not me. I believe if you've known someone, and you can haul yourself there, you should. Blame it on my DNA. Funeral-going is practically hereditary in my family thanks to my mum, Bernadette.

Now, Bernadette wasn't just a nurse; she was an overachiever in the funeral attendance department. She racked up so many, I swear she had a loyalty card. Twice, she even turned up at funerals for strangers. Not on purpose, mind. She'd simply gotten the time wrong, and by the time she realised she didn't recognise a single soul, she'd stay put—especially if the turnout was a bit thin. She figured the deceased deserved a few bonus prayers. That's Bernadette for you: part-time nurse, part-time stand-in mourner, and full-time giver of shifty side-eyes to anyone who dared leave before the service was over.

Then there's me and my mate Maureen. We took a slightly more recreational approach to cemeteries. Our routine was breakfast, then a casual browse among the gravestones. "Who's in and who's new?" was our little game. Sounds macabre, I know, but graveyards are like libraries—quiet, contemplative, and full of fascinating stories. Plus, as Bernadette used to say, "It's not the ones in the ground that'll do you harm; it's the buggers still breathing." Truer words have never been spoken.

Mum's expertise didn't end at funerals and pearls of wisdom. She also had a sideline in exorcisms. Yep, you heard me. If someone thought they had an unwelcome guest of the spectral variety, Bernadette would swing by, statue of Our Lady tucked under one arm, a bottle of Lourdes holy water in the other.

Her process was clinical: plonk the statue somewhere prominent, whip through a rosary like she was auditioning for the Vatican, and spritz the place with holy water until it smelled like a sanctified garden centre. She'd leave the statue behind for a week, in case the spirit needed more time to get the memo. And you know what? Nine times out of ten, it worked. The ghost moved on, or at least the homeowner convinced themselves it had, which, let's face it, is half the battle with these things.

So yeah, funerals, graveyards, and ghost-busting. It's all part of the family lore. And if Bernadette taught me anything, it's this: when life gets a bit too much, there's always a statue, some holy water, and a well-timed prayer to sort it all out.

That very statue braved the journey to Australia with me. Now, it sits pride of place next to my Death Box, candles often lit for anyone departing—or, frankly, anyone just having a rotten time of it. Our

Lady's still on duty, and Bernadette wouldn't have it any other way.

Every Christmas, I dutifully light a candle on top of it. Call it a ritual, twisted tradition if you like, but even the Reaper's got to show a bit of seasonal cheer for her clientele on the other side.

As someone entrusted with maintaining appearances, especially in the final weeks of a person's life, I became not just a stylist but a confidant, providing a neutral ground, the quiet space where they can speak their mind, even if it's just a mumbled complaint about the pudding in the nursing home.

Perdy needed round-the-clock care, so I made a separate trip to the nursing home to do her hair. It was a sad affair, not the light-hearted banter we used to have at the cottage. She was frail, a shadow of her former self, and that visit turned out to be the last time I would see her. She died shortly after.

As Perdy was laid to rest, I was asked by one of the sons if I could continue to cut Ted's hair. It was a simple request, and I agreed without hesitation. My instructions were to enter the cottage via a key code, and my payment would be waiting in an envelope on the sideboard. I would write the next appointment on the calendar, and this would be my new routine, a solitary task that felt both necessary and bittersweet. Today would be the first time I'd seen him since the funeral.

Walking into Ted's cottage on that day felt routine, yet sacred. I entered the cottage with my usual greeting of "Hi Ted and how are you?" I didn't expect a response, but a look of familiarity and a sad nod from him which spoke volumes was a good enough sign for me to engage and get started. Confined to his very comfortable-looking bed, he cut a lonely figure without his beloved Perdy, hair overgrown and awaiting a resurrection. But life goes on, I thought as I patted his hand with a cheerful "Good to see ya."

I thought it best to stay light-hearted and breeze through the next thirty minutes of restyling; Well, that is, until I found myself in a home salon saga like no other.

16

PUMP IT UP

ELVIS COSTELLO & THE ATTRACTIONS

I SET up my tools and pressed the brake release on the castors of the bed and manoeuvred it away from the wall. I popped the cutting cape around him which I draped over him at the head of the bed, making it easier to access him for his haircut and to vacuum afterwards. I grabbed my clippers and began shearing the back of Ted's head, his white hair, tumbling to the floor. I kept up a bit of chat, more for myself than him. I mentioned what a beautiful send-off Perdy had, but he just nodded as he focussed on the telly. His love for cricket was still alive and well, and I wasn't about to risk ruining that.

Five minutes in, as the telly droned on about wickets and overs in the background, something shifted in the room. Ted, usually, still as a statue, had started to twitch. Odd, I thought – he's normally the poster boy for stoic immobility. I figured maybe he was uncomfortable, so I upped my speed. The quicker I wrap this up, the better it is for both of us. His breathing suddenly changed and became heavier, followed by a cough like he was trying to clear his throat. A few seconds later, a deep inhale-exhale situation ensued. I asked if he was okay. No response. He seemed too calm, almost like he was daydreaming about his dear Perdy, so I carried on cutting.

Then, suddenly, his head jerked to one side, followed by his shoulder as he started to keel over to one side, like a wonky bookshelf.

I moved around the edge of the bed, my hairdresser instincts kicking in – Assess, adjust, and clip.

"You okay Ted?"

I asked again, a bit more urgently this time – it was like he wasn't aware of my presence. His eyes were glazed over in a fixated stare towards the foot of the bed. What was he looking at? Scanning the situation, my heart began to race as I realised something wasn't right. My inner voice screamed; He's having an attack! Call for help! But before I could reach for my phone, I noticed something ... unsettling.

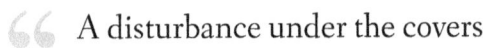 A disturbance under the covers.

This fluttering and jerking movement was at the hip level, and Ted's right arm was suspiciously missing and underneath the duvet. His left hand was visible on top, innocently resting.

I immediately stepped back trying to refocus my eyes. What was I looking at? Was I seeing this correctly? And then the noises started – grunts. Not the grunts of a man struggling with illness. Oh no. These were deep rhythmic grunts, of .... well, of a man whose mind was not on cricket.

The tugging under the covers got quicker and more determined like he was picking up the pace for the final lap in an invisible race. And there I was, pinned to the spot in frozen watchfulness. I was speechless as I watched him jerk in rhythm, nodding his head like he was at a rock concert, jamming out a song only he could hear.

My brain was doing cartwheels. Do I step in? Do I try to steady his balance, or let him topple over? I was torn between my instinct to help and my overwhelming desire to avoid getting dragged further into this situation. The last thing I needed was to add more excitement to this already unstoppable rally.

My heart pounded like a drum as the scene played out in front of me. I was rooted to the spot, trapped in a swirl of alarm and confusion. Every instinct screamed at me to move, to act, to do something but I was just glued to the spot as my stomach churned, nausea rising with every passing second, and I was stuck—caught between the urge to run and the desperate need to intervene.

No one had prepared me for this at hairdressing college.

As an unwilling observer, my head swam in blind panic as to how long the duration of this would last. I found myself amid a surreal sitcom situation with no laughing track, just the unsettling rhythm of a man in the throes of something far beyond my expertise. There were no words in this strange dance-off, just a thirty-something-year-old witnessing a ninety-something-year-old in an unrestrained sensual moment ... of, shall we say, enthusiasm. The sort of scene that might've ended with a discreet fade-to-black in a film, but I was stuck right in the middle of the climax, literally.

Finally, Ted let out the grunt of all grunts, deep and guttural, the kind that made me instinctively check my surroundings. And as if on cue, the cricket match on the telly reached its crescendo – someone hit a six. The crowd erupted in cheers, and that was that! It was over. Ted deflated like a sad bouncy castle, retreating into his supremely still self.

His stance screamed "astral traveller", like he'd just returned from some epic carpet ride across the universe and was trying to remember how gravity worked. I half expected him to snap out of it, rub his belly, and casually declare. "Oh, I'm back! Anyone else feel like a snack?"

Dilemma: Now, what do I do? Abandon the haircut or navigate the awkwardness. I stood there, clippers in hand, staring at the half-done head of hair. I had to think fast on my feet. I imagined calling upon his son, who lived next door, trying to explain why dad had half a haircut. Did he really need to know this, or the intricate details given Ted will need future haircuts?

Then the thought hit me: the carers would be arriving soon, bright and chipper, to check on him and maybe refresh his linen. What mess will they find? More than they signed up for, no doubt. What questions would this beg?

Ted may be bedridden, but his bed wasn't exactly at rest. I could only imagine their confusion, and "Why does he only have half a haircut?"

I took a deep breath. Dig deep, Liz! I thought to myself. What would my mum advise for a favourable outcome? Funny how we still hear the best advice from our mums even when they are no longer around.

> "Don't make a fuss, Elizabeth, be gracious and complete the job."

Classic Bernadette advice. And as much as I wanted to bolt out of the door, it was spot on.

With the professionalism I never knew I possessed, I finished the haircut, working swiftly, avoiding eye contact with anything below neck level. I patted him on the shoulder when I was done. "There you go, Ted. That should feel better!" as nonchalant as I could manage. I scribbled another appointment on the calendar, locked up the cottage, and left.

Back in the car, panicking, I frantically rang my friend Fiona, a registered nurse.

"Fiona, you've got to help me out here," I blurted. I then proceeded to spill every crude detail of what transpired with Ted, my voice dripping with concern. "I'm telling you, Fiona, the carers are going to follow me and find..... Well, I don't know what they will find! What if it's a sticky mess? Look, I need this documented. After all, I was alone with a man who was vulnerable, bedridden, and nearly One hundred years old. I don't want to end up on the evening news!"

Instead of offering sympathy as a true friend, Fiona burst into uncontrollable laughter. She assured me this was just a part of life's rich tapestry. After all, who could blame a ninety-seven-year-old for having such vitality?

And no worries, Sis, I'll document it, still howling at my embarrassing predicament.

But that's the thing about this job – it's never just about the hair. It's about the people, the stories, the lives that carry on even when everything seems to be slipping away.

Driving away, I pondered Perdy closing the gate behind me as she used to do when she was alive. Looking behind me in the rearview mirror, I imagined her approving nod and her familiar voice rang through my head.

Good Job, Lizzi.

17

HERE I GO AGAIN
WHITESNAKE

AS I PEELED out of Ted and Perdy's driveway, a vivid memory flashed. A reflective story from my salon days came into my focus, which, given current events, now made me smile and shake my head. I had worked in a few salons, but this story resonated mostly with my own place where I was part owner in the business. It was situated on a bustling high street, and beyond that, the area had a lively village feel.

Our salon was a slice of small-town heaven, where locals gathered to socialise, get their locks sorted, and soak up some good old-fashioned chit-chat. The down-to-earth atmosphere and friendly welcome were indeed our unique selling point. It was like the bar in the classic sitcom Cheers, but with more hairspray and fewer barstools. Laughter often spilt out of doors, which encouraged more people to join the 'Hair party.'

Newcomers would stroll in, wide-eyed and bedazzled by the cosy vibe. "I love how homely it feels here," they'd say, embracing the warm welcome. My response: "Great, cos we're busy. Go make yourself a cup of tea, and while you're at it grab the broom."

It worked every time.

Each new visitor wove themselves into the fabric of the place, getting swept quite literally into our little hair party. They all became regulars, whether they liked it or not. This was a simpler time – before mobile phones and the internet invaded our lives. Back then, your options during a haircut were limited to a magazine, a cup of tea, and a bit of gossip if you were lucky. And if you wanted an appointment, you'd have to walk into the salon or pick up the phone like a normal person. Cash and cheques ruled the day, and services were booked with a real live receptionist – no online bookings asking if you "agree to the terms and conditions" (not that anyone reads those).

With the right crowd in the salon, the atmosphere was always a blend of cosy and lively. I'd occasionally chime in with a story or two to keep the conversation flowing. One such story involved Jeff and a pre-holiday haircut. I knew they would bend their ear to a bit of gossip, some folks can't resist the allure of a juicy tale whether they are avid listeners, witty commentators, or self-appointed problem solvers.

> Egged on by the other stylists, I began laying out the dilemma I had with Jeff, a client's husband, visiting the salon for the first time.

My only personal encounter with Jeff prior was him popping his head through the salon door with a cheeky grin, asking, "Can you do anything with this?" while patting the patch of his scalp where his hairline used to be. Classic bloke humour of the time. My response? – I try to be God, but unfortunately ... with a deadpan, wry smile. We'd share a laugh, he'd disappear and that was that!

Honestly, you won't find a hairdresser alive who hasn't been hit with that tired quip by countless 'witty guys' over the years. As if hearing it for the hundredth time will somehow make it funnier ... It doesn't.

His wife Lesley was a regular with us and had decided to treat him to some salon pampering. Normally, he would hit up the local barber, but they'd just booked last–minute flights to Spain and he just needed a tidy-up. Lesley, in full "pre-holiday panic" mode, shoved him through the door as she dashed off to grab some currency (probably a well-deserved break from Jeff's banter). Her parting words, "Give him the works!"

Now, in those days, barber shops weren't exactly luxurious. No fancy gadgets, just a bloke in a white coat yielding clippers like a bomb disposal expert, one wrong move and you've got an accidental mohawk. But here in the salon, we were about luxury and relaxation, a spa day for your scalp. After shampooing Jeff's hair – what was left of it – he settled into the cutting chair like he was sinking into a beanbag. He swivelled the chair 360 degrees surveying this new environment. Bit posh in here, he chuckled, comparing the upmarket feel to the rugged charm of Shaky Pete's, his usual hair-cutting haunt.

Spray gun in hand, I began spritzing his remaining strands, but not before Jeff chimed in, grinning from ear to ear,

> "Oi, I'm not a plant, you know!"

Here we go! I thought he's here more about the banter than the trim. I braced myself for a comedy routine, but with my own sparkling wit, honed over seven years and always ready for battle, I instead steered the conversation to safer ground, Holidays.

As the clippers buzzed, Jeff launched into full holiday brag mode. They'd bought a new apartment in the Costa del Sol, and suddenly, he was a man of the world." Lesley's packed about five suitcases," he grumbled, rolling his eyes so far back, I'm surprised they didn't disappear altogether. I gave him a knowing look and some sage advice: "Never argue about wardrobe space, Jeff. It's a battleground no man ever wins." He chuckled, leaned in conspiratorially and winked. "We're planning to have friends over. Even the odd hairdresser, if they do a good job, eh?"

Smooth as butter, this one I thought. I raised an eyebrow, smirking to myself, thinking, good luck running that plan by Lesley.

As I began blending Jeff's top fluff to the sides, he began shuffling in his seat and leaning towards the mirror, squinting, turning his head at angles only an owl should attempt, nodding his approval. "That's good, that's good! You clearly know what you're doing!"

Pleased he was happy, I carried on, but again, the shuffling and squinting continued. Now, cutting a moving target is one thing, but dealing with chair dancing is another. I wasn't sure if this was just standard Jeff-ness. What I did know was I had stayed back late as a favour and needed this service to be straightforward as I had plans after work.

Saved by the salon phone ringing, I darted over to deal with an appointment, all the while keeping one eye on Jeff. That's when I noticed the Super shuffle had begun. Tilting to one side and now with his shoulder rolling, the cutting cape covering him was doing a jig like it had developed a mind of its own. He glanced over his shoulder as if to check to see where I was. Unbeknownst to him, I had a perfect view of his little performance through the mirror. Was he churning butter under there?

> Alone in the salon after hours, with a client's husband, my brain was flooded as to where this was going.

As the cape continued to dance and jive, my mind started racing to places I didn't want to go.

"Oi, Jeff!" I barked, with an authoritative tone to break his concentration. His head swivelled like an owl, giving me a dreamy glance, but still the dancing of the cape continued, his hands nowhere to be seen.

Quickly sizing the situation, it hit me like a freight train – he had crossed a line. I felt overwhelmed, caught between outrage and disbelief. It dawned on me that my youthful naivety had handed him the perfect opportunity to take advantage of my youthful naivety, all while I thought I was doing him a favour. But certainly not THAT kind of favour.

I approached him, brandishing my Denman hairbrush, which if you've never encountered one, is basically a small house brick with bristles. As I got closer, Jeff was smiling, completely oblivious to the fact that I was about to channel my inner ninja.

Then it happened. In a moment of sheer panic (and maybe just a smidge of overreaction),

I raised the brush and whacked Jeff clean on the forehead.

The satisfying swipe was followed by a "WHAT THeeeeeee—?" as he threw his hands up to shield himself from a second strike.... I may have slightly misjudged the pressure of the hit as it triggered a nosebleed that would make a vampire ravenous. With my heart racing and my sense of professionalism overtaken by horrified rage, I slapped a towel onto Jeff's face. His eyes were wide with incredulity. His smug grin, now replaced with the look of a man who'd been cornered by a wild animal.

At this point, as the storyteller to a salon full of clients, I could feel every single one of them mentally judging me, pinning me to the wall, hungry for the next sentence. All hair tools had been grounded. Clients were practically shoving their stylists to one side, like frantic midwives at a triple birth, barking Shhh!, to anyone who so much as breathed. Neck muscles strained as they craned for a better view, wide eyed, hands slapped over their mouths to muffle the shock-horror laughter bubbling up.

"I knoooooooow," I said.

Then his wife burst through the door like a tornado.

Cue Lesley.

"HEYYYYY"! she shouted before her voice trailed off, eyes bulging like she'd walked into an episode of —- CSI: — Salon.

There was Jeff, clutching a bloody towel to his face like he'd gone 10 rounds, toe-to-toe with Mike Tyson, and me, standing there with a brush in my hand, looking like a deer caught in the headlights.

Lesley's mouth hung open, her brain clearly working overtime to make sense of the scene. Her husband's bleeding!, me with a weapon! She needed answers – fast. But to be honest, so did I.

To bring clarity to the trauma I had just experienced, I ripped the cape off Jeff, in a panic, hoping to reveal...... I don't know, maybe a logical explanation? As his shirt unfurled, a pair of spectacles tumbled to the floor. As Jeff bent down, collecting them with a firm but shaky grasp, he mumbled,

"I was just cleaning my glasses. Wanted to see my haircut better."

As if that explained everything.

For a moment, I couldn't speak. My brain was doing some serious gymnastics trying to process the whole ordeal. I mean, what? Cleaning his glasses? I genuinely thought I'd caught him doing something.... well...let's just say .... INDECENT!

"I mean, how dirty can a pair of glasses be?"

Lesley, now clearly aware that the situation had escalated beyond belief, jumped in to calm the waters.

"Oooooh lovey, " she said in a tone that felt both reassuring and mildly condescending, "he'd never do anything like that," honouring the innocence on both sides of the situation and trying to smooth over the awkwardness.

I had the salon hanging onto my every word. Their faces were a glorious blend of suspense and confusion, as they teetered on the edge of this cliffhanger moment. I paused, holding the silence, smirking just enough to let them know I knew something they didn't.

"It was an innocent mistake," I said. From my angle, it looked like he was practically playing a banjo under that cape."

The room went quiet; but only for a second.....!

Then it hit! Rip-roaring laughter, like a dam bursting, the clients eating up the drama like it's a climax on their favourite soap.

Wide-eyed and in stitches, sipping their tea one minute, then choking and snorting it out of their noses the next. Not the best look for Maureen, but comedy gold, nonetheless. I could practically see the disbelief and joy fighting for space on their faces.

With a grin, I leaned back, "In all seriousness, though, it's put me in a real pickle – how much should I charge this guy? I'm running a business, not a laundry service! and now I've got extra towels to replace" More uproar. Irene was doubled over, practically begging for the outcome. You have to be joking! As she gasped for air. "Do we know these people, are they local?"

But in the end, like a plot twist no one saw coming, I dropped the bombshell.

> "Gotta tell ya, ladies … sorry, but … none of it is true!" I confessed, finally letting them off the hook. "I made it up!"

Silence.

Followed by more howling laughter and plaiting of legs.

Then howls of protest, refusing to accept this ordeal as fictitious and clamouring for more...

"Noooooo!" Joyce wailed, wiping tears away. "I so need this to be true!"

Meanwhile, the whole lot of them were shuffling, not so discreetly towards the bathroom. Age and gravity have no respect for a cup of tea, belly laughs and bladder control.

So, the legend of Jeff's' hair-raising adventure was born, forever cemented into salon folklore.

Little did I know this tale would serve as a perfect prelude to my own genuine, Ted experience. Moral of the story?

Be careful what you say in jest. Truth really is stranger than fiction.

And hey. If laughter is the best medicine, then consider this salon the ultimate prescription.

18

MAGICAL MYSTERY TOUR
THE BEATLES

ONE SUNNY DAY, my dad earmarked me for a trip to visit his Irish family in Huddersfield. Along for the ride was his brother Mick. Neither of them had seen their siblings in ages.

Imagine being one of twelve children. Yes, twelve. That's not a family; that's a small army. Sadly, two of the girls had died in infancy due to tuberculosis, but most were still alive and kicking among this battalion. As the clan had spread across the globe like a scattergram, four of the brothers had remained in Yorkshire, gathering all of them together with their offspring was a rare and special occasion.

Naturally, the task fell to me and my partner to chauffeur them. The journey was supposed to be a simple twenty-mile drive. Notice the emphasis on 'supposed'.

We set off, spirits high, cruising through the Yorkshire green belt, the sun pretending to be the best of British for a change. As we neared the destination, I sought more precise directions from my father.

With the authority of a man who had lived there for three decades, he confidently declared, "It's right at this roundabout."

I gave him a look – half bewildered, half amused, because the reality was,

"Dad, there is no right at this roundabout. You can only go left or straight across."

He squinted at the road ahead as if willing an extra exit into existence before offering his next nugget of navigational genius.

> "Well, the house is near a pub called... The.... Something," he said.

Well, that certainly narrows it down a bit. Who needs a map when you've got my dad's foggy recollections and Yorkshire's pub scene as your guide, narrowed down to pubs beginning with, The..

Directions: courtesy of the Irish Navigation Committee. They'd been in England for thirty years but couldn't direct a cow to pasture. So, we circled, and circled, and circled some more. We were practically locals by the time Dad finally recognized the street. Hallelujah.

We dropped them off at the designated house, which was already buzzing with Irish hospitality. Chairs were arranged around the room's edge, a typical Paddy's arena for social interaction. With our duty done, we left them to their merry reunion.

Three hours later, we returned to find the party in full Irish swing. Laughter echoed, stories flowed, and the air was thick with the scent of tea and whiskey. And of course, there was food. Piles of it. Heaps. It's an Irish gathering, after all, they're born feeders.

My partner and I sat patiently, mixing politely with the younger generation and waiting for the signal to depart. But that wasn't going to happen anytime soon. We were welcomed with open arms, mixing with cousins and the next generation, just in case we needed to recognise them at a future funeral or family meltdown.

That's when I heard a conversation that would ever be etched in my memory.

The Irish love their stories, especially the ones with questionable advice – and Dad was in full swing, holding court on a topic he thought was groundbreaking.

Dad, amidst a group of his brothers, was explaining his foolproof cure for bedwetting.

"I once cured bedwetting, with a mouse," he began, capturing everyone's attention. The room fell silent, all ears on Dad, eagerly awaiting this so-called wisdom.

> "I captured and killed a mouse, boiled it up in a pan and gave the water to my daughter."

He stated this, as casually as if he were discussing the secret ingredient in his famous stew.

My head whipped around, ears on full alert. "Which daughter?" I interjected, the blood draining from my face as I grabbed his leg in sheer panic.

"Angela, he replied, completely unfazed by my sudden death grip.

Relief washed over me like a tidal wave – Thank God it wasn't me. But the horror wasn't over. "Dad, are you serious? You can't be serious", I stammered, desperately hoping this was one of those tall Irish tales.

But no, Dad nodded with the nonchalance of someone discussing the weather.

"Oh, I'm serious. I got the cure from my father-in-law. I killed the little mouse myself, cleaned it, and boiled it. There was no disease, it was perfectly safe.

Perfectly safe. Because boiled mouse water is the hallmark of safety.

My brain was struggling to keep up with the sheer lunacy of it all. I asked again, "Wait, "You killed the mouse, boiled it up and gave the water to my sister?"

He nodded; his confidence unwavering." It worked, didn't it? "It cured the problem.

Now, I'm no expert, but I'm pretty sure, boiling a mouse to cure bed wetting isn't in the parenting manual, and he was offering it up like it was a cup of Horlicks before bed. To everyone else in the room, it was a borderline confession to child endangerment. We sat there in stunned silence, collectively wondering if we should phone a doctor or perhaps a solicitor.

Later, at home, I couldn't wait to tell Mum about Dad's latest venture into the realms of insanity, especially the part where her own father was the mastermind behind it.

Her face paled as she took it all in. Another notch on the bedpost of Dad's wild ideas she had no part in. "Don't tell Angela, she said, her voice tinged with the weariness of someone who'd seen it all. She'll be disturbed."

> Disturbed? That was the understatement of the century.

But Mum, like the rest of us, had long resigned herself to the circus that was our home, where sanity was optional, and laughter was mandatory. That being said... Sometime after Dad's infamous announcement about his rodent-based remedy for childhood bedwetting, I thought a little research was in order.

What Matty called an ancient remedy, the rest of us called the deranged ramblings of a man one bolt away from a padded room. It wasn't just absurd or outlandish – it was the kind of suggestion that made you rethink every pot of stew he had ever offered you.

Turns out, this ancient recipe wasn't one of Matty's side experiments, this little gem had pedigree. This particular nugget of medical wisdom was a hand-me-down, not the garden variety like "here's your grandads watch" sort of heirloom. But through countless generations, from the well-read mind of a noble Roman citizen. Its original creator? Pliny the Elder, an ancient Roman polymath and all-around overachiever, who is credited with penning Naturalis Historia – essentially the world's first encyclopaedia, and, apparently, an unofficial guide to home-brewed horrors.

Through the aeons of time and the patchwork of geography, this cure for bed-wetting and banishing childhood nervousness, somehow found itself lodged in the head of Matty – a part-time philosopher, full-time Irish crane driver, and proud Yorkshire resident with a shaky reliance on the NHS and Big Pharma.

Pliny was a well-travelled and astonishingly educated man of his time. You'd think someone with his resume would aim a little higher than " boil a rodent and drink it"

This peculiar lineage of knowledge goes a long way to explaining Matty's unnerving casual, matter-of-fact delivery when he dropped the rodent bombshell on everyone that day.

To Matty, it was a time-tested, historically backed remedy with a touch of Roman gravitas.

So there you have it: Dad wasn't so much an unhinged inventor as a loyal student of ancient insanity. I'm just relieved that Matty didn't follow Pliny the Elder's 'recipe' to the letter, which required the afflicted child to eat the boiled mouse.

The thought of Bernadette walking into the kitchen and stumbling into the scene of Angela sitting at the dinner table, staring in sheer horror at a boiled mouse in the centre of her dinner plate, broiled in the embers of the kitchen fire, no doubt. Dad stood next to her, casually sharpening a huge carving knife with a sharpening steel, "So Angela, "leg or tail?" I know with absolute certainty if that had happened, it would have been Matty taking a stretcher ride to the hospital.

And where would Bernadette be? Cooling her heels off in the local police cells, calmly explaining to the officer on duty, 'He served our daughter a mouse for dinner, so I served him a skillet to the head. Fair's fair, isn't it?"

And let's be honest.

I'm sure those officers would nod in grim agreement-because let's face it, Bernadette wasn't exactly the type to blend into the wallpaper. Most of their prior dealings might've been over the phone and strictly " Matty matters" but you can bet, her voice alone would have left a mark.

19

WE DON'T HAVE TO TAKE OUR CLOTHES OFF

JERMAINE STEWART

LET'S rewind to the early days when I was a young Debutante on the dating scene.

You remember the days, don't you? Before swiping right and ghosting became the norm. Back when you actually had to try? It was a simpler time. If you fancied someone, you didn't just get away with just liking the photo, you had to engage your mouth, say hello, and hope that they weren't a total nutjob.

Attraction grew in real time with a bit of chemistry and a cheeky smile, numbers were exchanged. Home numbers. You remember those? Where the phone was plugged into the wall, with a turn dial, a receiver and a dangly chord.

If your house was a bit posh, you would have a second phone upstairs too, so some element of privacy on a call. Every minute added a few more pence to your bill, so you didn't waste time. If you had more to say, you popped around to see them for a further chat.

And then there was the party line, a lottery of sorts. You'd pick up the receiver, only to be dropped into the middle of someone else's chat, basically eavesdropping on some local gossip. So, you'd hang up, wait a bit, then try again hoping for a clear line. And if you had a house phone but no one to call? There was always the speaking clock "At the third stroke, it will be…

Communicating wasn't as simple as texting, oh no. You had to ring their house, and nine times out of ten, their mum or dad would answer. You'd have to charm your way through that gate keeper just to have a conversation.

If that conversation didn't make you run to the hills, you knew the other person was probably worth a chance. Dates happened, and by week four, you'd already met each other's families and mates. It was effort, it was intention, and if it fizzled out, no harm done. You moved on and waited for the next bloke brave enough to ring your landline.

Dating was a time honoured tradition. You'd lock eyes in a pub, give each other the 360-degree once-over, before he sidled up for a chat to test the waters. If he wasn't a total muppet, numbers were exchanged, and a date was set. He would drive over, knock on your door, and in my case, I invited him in to say a quick hello to my mum. Not because she cared too much at that point, but so she could clock the potential serial killer I'd be disappearing with, just in case she had to give a description to the police. Romance at its finest really.

After a nice dinner, he'd drop me home, all gentleman-like. Communication was smooth, further dates stacked up, and before you knew it, we were a proper couple. That slow-burn approach had more charm and required genuine effort. It was a test of your honesty – both to your prospective partner and yourself. And currently? People are treating dates like a pick-n-mix counter. They just can't decide if they want a soft or hard centre, take a quick bite, then hastily chuck it back on the shelf because they've just spotted another lolly to try.

Nowadays, the conversion rate of potential relationships making it to a more permanent situation is dismal, and if you haven't crashed and burned within three weeks, you're practically dating a unicorn.

So, where did it all go wrong? Well, hello internet. Now instead of introducing yourself at the bar, you can just match with someone on a dating app. Sounds efficient, doesn't it? Except now you're stuck with situationships with people who wouldn't have made it past the first face-to-face interaction back in the day.

If there was an argument back then, you couldn't just send a half-arsed "Sorry babe, love you really xx" and be back in the good books. Oh no, unless you were willing to wait for a chance meeting, you had to go knock on their door, and potentially face their parents. Imagine the horror.

> These days, relationships are disposable.

Break up? Patch it up via text. Want to end it? Just stop replying. It's that easy, and utterly rubbish. How times have changed.

But moving on.... Once upon a time in the rugged land of Yorkshire, where the tea is strong, and the weather is stronger, I found myself newly divorced and dipping my toes in the murky waters of online dating. Now I couldn't tell you which dating site I signed up for, it doesn't really matter, does it? It was 2013. People wrote themselves well in their profiles. They're all the same in the end: one fuzzy photo that looks like it was taken from space and chat-up lines so dodgy you'd think they were working undercover.

A few years prior to my introduction to online dating, my sister and her hubby ran an Elite dating agency – the sort where you had to have a job title with more syllables than "plumber" to even get a foot in the door. They matched businessmen with businesswomen, using criteria as exacting as a Michelin-star chef's recipe.

Back then, the only catfishing you had to worry about was someone turning up without a tie. People took it seriously; after all, they were investing in themselves, and serious about finding their "forever person". I was in an exclusive relationship at the time, but when we visited my sister for the weekend, I couldn't resist having a peek in the brochure of male clients, or the 'Man-alogue', as I called it, purely for entertainment purposes of course…

My sister was the chief matchmaker, whilst her partner took charge of signing them up . It was an assorted parade of hopefuls that could have doubled as a casting call for a summer cruising catalogue – or possibly a knitting pattern shoot. There were the odd one or two looking like candidates for next week's edition of TV's Crimewatch, and finally, a face only a mother could love, generously described as 'attractive.'

Fast forward a few years, and the whole world's dating habits were upended by the internet, flattening the old ways and slashing prices to encourage the masses. Suddenly everyone's swiping left and right like they're in a bloody martial arts film.

With the brave new world of matchmaking sites, people could showcase themselves in all their questionable glory. It was all about the visuals. People would carefully select and upload photos, and by "carefully" I mean they'd pick a photo from a decade ago, back when they still had their hair and a waistline.

I mean anything from their best friend's wedding in 2005 to a strategically cropped image that cut out their beer belly but not the beer. The usual stats were still there – height, hair and eye colour, smoker or non-smoker, kids or no kids – but honesty? That was optional, especially when it came to height. If I had a pound for every guy who claimed to be 6'2" but turned out to be about as tall as my Nana's garden gnome, I could've bought a small set of steps for them to stand on.

You had to be savvy, because who wants to spend an evening getting dolled up only to realise you've been catfished by someone who was more fiction than fact?

> Picture galleries were a real treat, too. It was a parade of lads showing off the one decent-sized fish they caught in 1998.

This has to be the saddest example of phallic wishing ever. Or cradling beers like they were Olympic trophies (parading their battle with alcoholism). Add in the guy lying shirtless on a bed like some Poundland version of Burt Reynolds. The aviator sunglasses made it impossible to see if he had eyes or was just into 1980s Top Gun cosplay.

And let's not forget the puppies – every other bloke had a cute dog in his profile like that was going to make me overlook the fact he hadn't seen a gym in the last decade.

And then there were the stories – the endless sagas about crazy exes, as if I was supposed to feel honoured to be the next participant on that nightmare roller coaster, Oh please!

And let's be perfectly clear. If you think I'm showing up with an overnight bag, you've got another thing coming. And by "another thing", I mean a hard pass, mate. Throwaway lines like, "We're adults aren't we?" as if that was some kind of Jedi mind trick to get me over the finishing line.

Or," Oh no, really, you take the bed – I'll be fine on the sofa."

This guy is about as convincing as a comb-over in a hurricane. You just know he'll be lying there fully clothed for about three seconds before the accidental migration back to the bed begins. Nice try, champ.

I wasn't in the market for emotionally stunted men, thanks very much. Speaking of which, let's talk about the ones who aren't just looking for a girlfriend – they're looking for a live-in carer, offering sponge baths would be an advantage.

Case in point: One charming chap who uploaded a profile picture from a hospital bed. Yep, there he was, hooked up to a drip. Because nothing says "ready to mingle" quite like a selfie from A&E.

At that point, I wondered if I was dating or being scouted by the NHS.

After sifting through the usual suspects, I struck up a bit of a rapport with a guy named Jim. He lived down south, but his job as an accountant for a large firm brought him up north on a weekly basis. Could he be my romantic commuter? His roots were firmly planted in southern soil, while I was very much a northern lass. Realistically, we didn't seem like much of a match, but we got on well enough when chatting, so why not?

20

SHOULD I STAY OR SHOULD I GO
THE CLASH

AS A HAIRDRESSER, I've heard all the stories. No one relishes joining a dating site. It's a necessary evil, like paying taxes or pretending to enjoy kale.

Months passed, and we met in person one day after a riveting chat about the weather. Nothing fancy, just a relaxed "Hello, how are you?" And let's see if you look anything like your profile picture, kind of affair. Besides, since my recent divorce, it had been a while since I'd been on a date that didn't involve a judge and a settlement agreement.

Jim and I agreed to meet at a hotel bar just off the motorway. I rolled into the carpark at 7.30 pm, which was the peak "awkward online date" time across the globe. I circled the car park, searching for a spot that didn't require a 5-point turn or divine intervention. The sun was making its final bow into a murky twilight that made everyone look ten years younger, or maybe that's just wishful thinking.

As I stepped out of my shiny new white cabriolet, my hard-earned prize from the divorce fairy – there he was.

"Nice wheels", he said with a smile of admiration. He embraced me with a half-handshake, half-hug combo.

"Thank you," I replied as I eyed up his working attire.

A suit, sharp enough to crunch numbers but not too sharp to offend the boss. With pleasantries out of the way, we strolled towards the hotel entrance, making small talk about the weather and traffic.

The bar was busy, two rows deep, with people jostling for drinks, so we joined the queue, making small talk. He offered me a drink, and I sensibly requested a small glass of wine. After all, our online chat had been the draw in the first place, but in real time, you never know how long these things will last.

You don't want to be nursing a large one when you realise your date has the conversational skills of a toaster.

Just as we were about to order, he glanced down at his phone. I noticed he had one of those "I'm going to be late for my train," looks on his face, only it wasn't a train. He was studying this alert on his phone. He kept glancing at it, then back at me, as if he was trying to solve a particularly tricky conundrum.

I was wondering if he was starting to have second thoughts. Was he contemplating a hasty exit, maybe one of those prearranged emergency texts? You know the type: "Oh, my sister has run out of baby milk," or "I've just remembered, I'm a keynote speaker at a conference in 30 minutes."

Then, before I could ask if everything was alright, he grabbed me and said, "Can we step to one side for a minute?" We moved to the hotel vestibule – very romantic, I know, where he then asked, "Are you Catherine?"

"Er, no, I'm Liz," I replied, now thoroughly perplexed. "Are you Jim?"

"No," he said with a sheepish grin. "I'm Robert."

Ah, Robert.

Apparently, Catherine had just arrived and was waiting in the car park to meet him.

Wide-eyed panic immediately transformed into a short bout of mutual laughter. "You better go then," I said, as we quickly wished each other well, and he scurried off to meet Catherine. I sauntered back to the car, wondering if this sort of mix-up happened to other people or if I was exceptionally gifted in the art of romantic disaster.

Just then, my phone buzzed with the message from Jim, who was running late but had finally arrived. I had the distinct pleasure of explaining to him how I'd just waltzed off into the bar with an absolute stranger, mistaking him for the real Jim. He looked confused, which, honestly, was the least of my worries at that point. I was more concerned with finding a way to slip into the pub without drawing any attention – or, heaven forbid, running into Robert and Catherine.

The thought of Jim and me sidling up to the same bar, served by the same member of staff who had clocked me a mere ten minutes ago, filled me with a sense of impending doom. I could already see it – his inevitable double-take, the flicker of recognition as he pieced it together: "Well, she doesn't hang about, does she?"

Followed by his wry grin and cheeky wink.

> "Good evening again, madam. I wasn't aware the Speed Dating club had booked a table tonight".

Would you like a stopwatch with your G & T – made me cringe a little.

Luckily, Jim and I managed to find a secluded spot, away from the prying eyes of anyone who might have seen me swanning around with two different men in one evening. The irony, of course, is that in the early days of online dating, all we had to go on was foggy pixelated photos. You never really knew who you were going to meet, so focused on the green flags and hoped for the best.

It was a bit like standing at a bus stop, squinting as the bus lumbers towards you. You're trying to make out the destination number, wondering if it's the one you need, or just another bus leading to nowhere useful. So, you half-heartedly stick your arm out, trying to gauge if anyone else is going to make a move because heaven forbid you commit to a wave for the wrong bus. As it pulls up, you're praying it's your bus. No one wants that exasperated look from the bus driver when you sheepishly realise you've flagged down the wrong bus, then sheepishly shuffle back to the anonymity of the bus shelter.

In hindsight, Robert looked nothing like Jim. Jim had dark hair; Robert's was mousey brown and paired with the added spectacles which screamed, "Milky bar kid." But when a man approaches you with such confidence as you're stepping out of your car, you just assume he's the one you're meant to meet. Perception can be a funny thing, especially when you are trying to make sense of the dating world.

But at least both Robert and Jim told me I had nice hair. We hairdressers hear that a lot, after all.

Conclusion – Online dating is less about finding Mr. Right, and more about dodging, Mr. What was I thinking?

Now - onto another delicate subject.

Friends with Benefits – the modern-day fairy tale where Prince Charming shows up without flowers but promises he'll text you back. I know, I know, a controversial subject, but let me tell you, I've had plenty of clients sit in my chair who initially thought this setup was a stroke of genius. No strings, no drama, just fun, right?

Until one of them develops feelings – the uninvited guest to the no-strings party. That's when the whole thing goes from casual to complicated to catastrophic, ending in tears and regret.

Who came up with that? It's like playing some tragic version of Monopoly where you get to visit all the houses but never buy the bloody thing. No attachment, no investment, just falsehoods from someone who'll string you along like you're auditioning for a role that doesn't exist.

What are the benefits, exactly?

Are they coming around to fit you in a kitchen?

Are they laying you a new patio? No, they are not.

Ladies, listen up: You are not in the sale!

If he wants you, he better be paying full price.

This casual fling malarkey is like blocking the entrance to the driveway to someone who actually sees your value – and who might – JUST MIGHT, be willing to install that bloody kitchen. And if you do meet a guy who seems to be ticking your boxes, here's my top tip: speak to him regularly and between 5 and 8 pm. That's prime time, love. If he's "too busy" to chat between those hours, pack it in and move on. Don't waste your time with someone who's too distracted for the basics. You deserve more than someone who comes alive at 11 pm with a, "u up?" text.

Remember, love is like a good haircut. If it looks like you did it yourself, it's probably not working. Now don't get me wrong, I'm no prude. I do make a special exception for women over a certain age, let's say over sixty-five. Those ladies have earned their stripes and then some. They love to throw me a cheeky wink and say" Hey Liz, I've got a friend with benefits.

Buried too many husbands – just keeping it simple now." At that stage of life, it's basically "grab what you can love, and if it makes you smile, even better." But, let me be clear, that rule only applies to women who've lived long enough to tell a few stories of their own.

Now that's my big sister chat done for the day. Take it or leave it – but I suggest you take it.

21

BIG LOVE
FLEETWOOD MAC

The Dark One - Part 1

I REFUSE to give him a name, for to utter it would grant him power he does not deserve. Instead, I simply refer to him as "the dark one" – a fitting moniker for a person shrouded in deceit and deception. He hides behind a borrowed name, a pathetic attempt at originality that only serves to emphasise his lack thereof, a name lifted from a relative.

The day I responded to that message on social media was the day I unwittingly stepped onto a rollercoaster ride of emotions. At times, I look back and rue that decision, but on most days, I choose to see it as a lesson. A lesson that taught me more about myself than I ever thought possible.

It all started innocently enough. I had recently moved house, surrounded by boxes still waiting to be unpacked, and Christmas decorations lingering in the corners of the room. It was a winter evening, and I was elbow-deep in dishwater when a notification flashed across my phone screen. It was a guy I had known in my youth, a blast from the past, reaching out with a friendly note of engagement.

What followed were hours of fun and entertaining text exchanges that made me forget about the dishes waiting to be dried. He was living overseas, divorced like me, had three grown-up children, and was full of enthusiasm in sharing the updates on his life so far.

It was nice to catch up, but with the time zone difference of twelve hours and bedtime looming, I wound the conversation down, said goodnight and headed off to bed.

Woken by an early morning phone call from him the next day, our brief catch-ups quickly snowballed into daily chats. Before I knew it, we were diving into deep conversations. He mentioned visiting relatives in Europe in a few months, and suddenly, the possibility of meeting in person didn't seem so far-fetched.

Each day, as we navigated around our busy schedules, juggling work and family life, we found ourselves drawn closer together. Every spare minute he had was spent texting or Face Timing me, and despite the three decades that had slipped by, it felt as though time had simply dissolved. As we chatted, I couldn't help but feel a spark of excitement at the prospect of rekindling an old connection. He filled me in on his life. A lengthy marriage that had yielded children, but in the end, led to a conclusion.

> Sporting the boyish grin I remember, he stood at five feet, nine inches, boasting a full head of grey hair, the same blue eyes I remember, and a complete set of teeth – such a bonus!

Our FaceTime chats were frequent and engaging, and voice calls were a daily staple. As a manager in a firm, he'd often chat from his office, making time during his busy day. You know how people sometimes worry about the pace of communication at the start of a relationship?

They wonder if those gaps in conversation or communication are red flags – signs of disinterest, or worse, they are just being strung along for attention. No one wants to seem needy, but let's face it. When those texts or calls don't come, it's hard not to overthink.

But here I was, with a guy who was as far away as he could be, and yet there were no gaps. Not one. It felt like real progress, a sense that maybe this time things would be different. He was making plans to be with me, building an itinerary, and my inbox was overflowing. It was as if he was determined to erase the distance between us one message at a time. And honestly, it was working.

Before I knew it, we were in the middle of a whirlwind romance, and marriage was potentially on the table for us. After in-depth discussions about our previous relationships and experiences, I found myself swept up in the idea of a happily ever after. Five months later, I found myself at the airport waiting for his plane to land.

We knew the landing time would be tight, as I raced there right after my school run. I had just parked and was rearranging my boot for his suitcase when out of nowhere, I was suddenly grabbed from behind. Naturally, I jumped and let out a girly squeal. Before I could react, he swirled me around, pulled me close, and planted a smacker right on my lips. That boyish charm of his was still very much alive as we embraced in a long, warm hug.

The car ride home buzzed with nervous excitement, like two teenagers on a first date. We decided to make a pit stop at a pub for a drink – an excuse to have a proper chat and soak in the moment. But, the bottom line was, that we were both over the moon to be together, like two pieces of a puzzle that had been missing far too long.

Now back on English soil, we spent time cementing our relationship in the flesh – no more pixelated promises over FaceTime. A trip to Europe was on the horizon, where my girls and I would be introduced to his parents, all while soaking up the sun and building bonds for the future. It felt like the start of something truly special, a blending of families under the Mediterranean sun. Upon our return to Yorkshire, we gathered our nearest and dearest for a small, cosy wedding day. The celebrations went without a hitch, as if the universe itself had given us its blessing. We were finally starting our new chapter.

Our next stop was a trip overseas with my two daughters to visit him in his place in New Zealand.

We were in discussions and testing the means to move to New Zealand, but with our original agreement, we decided he would ultimately move to England if that wasn't an option. We could always revisit the plan later.

His bungalow was perched on a peninsula, just a thirty-minute drive from the city, nestled into a hillside, close to the water, boasting a cosy log-burning fire. He'd moved to this larger space to accommodate us as a family. With an action-packed itinerary, there was plenty to keep us busy, with rest days carefully sprinkled in between. The trip started beautifully, with skiing being the highlight of our adventure. We travelled around the South Island, soaking up its stunning views and magnificent landscapes – truly a slice of heaven. Fun filled the days on the slopes at various ski resorts, however, as the saying goes, all that glitters is not gold.

I appreciated the plans he had put in place for our trip, but it soon became apparent that he wasn't the cool, calm travel planner he claimed to be.

It all started with a seemingly harmless disagreement over navigating foreign toilets in a bustling ski resort. We were searching for a loo for my young girls. A straightforward task, or so I naively thought. But no, he decided it was time to whip out the GPS and turn a quick bathroom search into a whole expedition. Meanwhile, the girls were doing the potty dance, and I wasn't about to wait for him to locate the toilets by satellite. So, I did the unthinkable.

I asked a passer-by for directions.

22

THE VOICE WITHIN
CHRISTINA AGUILERA

WELL, you'd have thought I'd committed a cardinal sin. My crime? Not waiting for his coordinates to magically appear.

"I was sorting it!" he barked, clearly wounded that I'd dared to take practical action. Little did I know, this affront to his manly sense of direction was just the first in a series of plot twists I was entirely unprepared for. Hardly surprising, considering some of his credentials were accredited by the University of Photoshop.

Now this was a man who firmly believed that if he saw something done once, he could master it. He had a certain confidence that bordered on delusion. I realised the extent of his self-assurance and highly questionable ethics during a visit to his office, where he proudly asked me to spot the fake certificates on his office wall, each one proclaiming his supposed expertise in various fields.

To say I was taken aback would be an understatement. But he just gave a knowing giggle, as if cheating the system was some sort of inside joke. The crazy thing was, he pulled it off. He was competent, no doubt about it, and people took him at face value, never questioning his capabilities. He'd simply found himself a fast track, bypassing the hassles of legitimate courses, and somehow, no one seemed to notice, or even care.

Skiing was no exception to his "see it once, nail it for life" philosophy. After a handful of lessons under his belt, he was convinced he was ready to tackle the slopes like a pro. Naturally, he also assumed that I, as an intermediate skier, would be thrilled to nurture his burgeoning talent, so we could glide gracefully down the mountainside together while the girls were tucked away in ski school. It was a lovely idea – on paper. I naively believed we could share this experience. What I didn't anticipate was him losing control, careening down the mountain like a runaway snowman, crashing into a safety barrier and impaling himself on his ski pole.

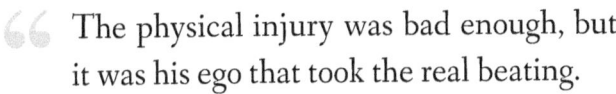
> The physical injury was bad enough, but it was his ego that took the real beating.

I could see the hurt pride simmering beneath the surface, and his mood dipped even lower than before. I suggested we call it a day, and make our way back to his place, but once back, the fallout wasn't over. No, he still had a bone to pick, yet again, about my so-called, "disrespect" about asking strangers for directions.

We argued about practicality versus pride, about when a kid needs a loo, you just find the nearest bathroom and go. But my logic fell on deaf ears, and before I knew it, he was gone. Just poof! Disappeared.

His car vanished down the driveway, gravel crunching under the tyres as he sped away. No note. No text, not even a breadcrumb trail to follow.

There I was, stranded in the middle of nowhere, with no transport with my girls, and nothing but nature walks to distract me from this bewildering fiasco. I naturally told the girls; that he had gone to work.

By the next lunchtime, there he was as if he'd just popped out for a pint of milk, completely unfazed.

He reappeared, all apologetic and contrite, and I, ever the optimist, bought it, chalking it up to stress. New relationship jitters, surely. We'd kiss, make up, and vow to start afresh. Because that's what healthy couples do, right? They grow, they learn, they argue over pastries and then grow some more.

Except, we weren't growing. At least not in any healthy direction. One day we were blissfully planning our future, the next he would be accusing me of God knows what. An argument would flare up from nowhere, leaving me scratching my head as none of it made sense.

I soon learned; that his Houdini act would become a recurring theme. His magical disappearances became as predictable as my frantic attempts to rationalise them. Each time, I'd panic, ringing and texting to find out where he'd gone and when – or if – he was coming back. Over time, it became clear that this wasn't just a quirky habit but a calculated punishment, a message that I was to toe the line and not dare to challenge him.

The initial problems surfaced six months in, but by the twelve-month mark, the pendulum started to swing wildly in opposite directions.

> One moment, we felt a pure connection; the next, I had no idea where he was, worrying he was lying in a hospital somewhere, or what I'd done wrong.

A relaxed conversation could suddenly take a sharp turn into a stony silence, with him declaring that he thought I didn't care about him. The constant reassurance he needed felt like being pulled over a cliff.

He promised that moving to England would solve everything. Ah yes, the grand relocation plan – our salvation! He'd find a job, we'd settle into domestic bliss, and all would be well. Or so I let myself believe.

Once in England, I did everything I could to help him to adjust. I became his personal cheerleader, therapist, and career coach, all rolled into one. But the theme of our time together seemed to be one of self-sabotage. His pursuit for the right job never came to fruition, just lofty ideas about exploring a pub venture and then him changing his mind yet again. He insisted on carving a new career path now he was on home soil, but didn't appear to have a clear idea of what that would look like.

Any attempt at a buoyant mood or well-laid plan on my part would spark off a mood swing. If I dared to look too happy, he'd swoop in with a reality check. "Just because you're happy doesn't mean I am." It became clear that in this relationship, happiness wasn't a shared experience; it was a competition, and I was definitely on the losing team.

Eventually, the frustration reached boiling point.

He just wasn't being serious, was he? Not about his career, not about us, and certainly not about making a life together. The final straw came when he announced, out of the blue, that he needed to "earn some real money," and promptly hopped back on a plane to New Zealand.

Being with this man was like trying to hold onto a gust of wind – impossible, exhausting and ultimately, pointless.

Deep down, I knew something had to give. It was a slow realisation that our union was not being taken seriously by him – a realisation that shattered the illusions I had built up in my mind. But the truth, as it often does, eventually caught up with me. I had been picking up the pieces of a relationship that had been doomed from the start.

Amid all this turmoil, I found solace in my work, which was always a reliable distraction, and my role as a mother. I think he sensed a shift in me, a dwindling of hope that no amount of his antics could ignore. The timing couldn't have been worse – my sister had just been diagnosed with cancer. It was caught early, but an operation and possibly further treatments were needed. With my energies now focused elsewhere, he seemed to realise he was slipping out of my priority list. So, in a bid to stay relevant, he booked another flight for a visit in five weeks, as if that would somehow keep him at the centre of my universe.

We kept up communication, but my gut feeling refused to let me settle. Why was he so keen on jumping ship back to New Zealand?....... being so far away meant he wasn't easy to keep tabs on. My survival instinct kicked in, coupled with a sixth sense that drove me on my fact-finding mission.

Where do I start?

23

MAMBO NO.5 (A LITTLE BIT OF...)
LOU BEGA

> This hairdressing lady turned Scotland Yard detective overnight.

Step One:

SATELLITE NAVIGATION WAS my first port of call, which enabled his location on his phone, an oversight on his part, but a goldmine for me. All it took was a tap on his location icon on my phone, and there he was, pinpointed down to within twenty metres. As I cross-referenced his reported travels, the places he claimed to be visiting didn't match up with the real-time GPS pings. Instead of being at work, the map was dotted with places that screamed, "up to no good."

The more I dug, the deeper the rabbit hole went. His charming stories started to unravel, revealing a tangled web of lies and deceit. There were discrepancies in his whereabouts to suspicious "friendships" with other women, which he quickly brushed off as casual acquaintances. Even an ex-girlfriend had reappeared back on the scene. He downplayed it all, of course, assuring me this was long since extinguished. But my instincts told me otherwise.

Now, I'm not one to get insecure over the opposite sex. I work with everyone – men, women, and those who can't decide – and I've had male friends that go back decades. However, bottom line, I was legally bound to a man who had nothing to lose and everything to hide. Realising the mess I was in, I turned to the universe for help. I needed some divine guidance and strength to navigate this inevitable rocky road ahead.

At this point, I was satisfied I'd given him every opportunity to prove himself, and he'd taken each one to show his true colours. My fact-finding mission needed to be swift and precise

As someone who's always championed leaving toxic relationships and situations as far away in the rearview mirror as possible, I found myself in unfamiliar territory. I was now playing the role of detective in the mystery of my own marriage. It was a difficult and lonely journey, but technology became my invaluable ally in uncovering the harsh truth of the reality that I had been blindly living in, one forced upon me without my consent.

One fateful day, while logging out of a social media app on a spare tablet, an unexpected option to log in with a preset password appeared.

A password belonging to another user. With a few clicks, a flood of current clandestine conversations between my husband and his ex-girlfriend came to light. He played the role of the pursuer, while she toyed with him like a cat with a ball of yarn. His messages portrayed me in a negative light, painting me as an unbalanced individual.

Despite the emotional blow, I resolved to separate my "detective self" from my predicament as a distressed overseas wife.

A week later, I found myself deep in the murky depths of Facebook where I accidentally stumbled upon a section of filtered messages I never knew existed.

There, like a grim treasure chest, I unearthed

messages from a woman in New Zealand, meant for me.

In her painfully detailed account, she revealed herself as my husband's girlfriend until the day he abruptly vanished. Spinning elaborate lies about his dying father in Europe. With heartbreaking honesty, she offered photos as proof of them together. She had even driven him to the airport, where he had paused under a streetlight, and posed with her for one last photo as a keepsake till he returned.

But instead of grieving for a father who was nowhere near death's door, he had married me. This revelation shattered her, and she reached out to me in confusion and despair.

However, the messages had sat there, unread for eighteen months. I had uncovered them far too late to prevent the deception for either of us. She had been promised a special weekend away upon his return, an event that would never happen.

> The shock of her story chilled me to the bone, as I realised the true nature of the man I was attached to.

A man with no moral compass, no soul, who could easily serve up lies about his family. And as far as I know, his father is still very much alive and well, just another casualty of his endless deceit.

Armed with this newfound knowledge, I reached out to her to piece together the puzzle of his deceitful actions. Together, we uncovered a pattern of lies and manipulation that painted a disturbing portrait of the stranger I had married. She had dodged a bullet, and I had been stabbed in the back!

As his return to England loomed just a month away, I transitioned from a passive observer into a private investigator. Emboldened, I refused to become another pawn in his personal, twisted, game of Relationship Chess. Where he believed he held all the pieces but was blissfully unaware he'd met a queen he couldn't topple.

I resolved to conduct some proactive plotting, eager to orchestrate some surprises of my own. It was clear that what I had glimpsed was just the tip of the iceberg. His insatiable appetite for female attention was glaringly evident. His ego knew no bounds.

From flirtatious messages with an ex to casually abandoning another unsuspecting woman, he left a trail of confusion and broken hearts in his wake.

It was clear this "situationship" was heading straight for the legal battlefield, and I needed the "tea" on him – and piping hot. There was no way I was going to let a few thousand miles, or his slippery ways, keep me from uncovering the truth.

Step Two:

So, with a dash of creativity, I set up an online dating profile in his region. With a bit of sleuthing, I fine-tuned the search parameters to zero in on our not-so-prince charming. And wouldn't you know it, Lady Luck smiled upon me as I stumbled upon a profile, devoid of a picture (how very mysterious) but teeming with tantalising clues to confirm it was him. With the assistance of cut & paste, I gathered a few carefully selected photos and set the trap. It was time for the hunter to become the hunted.

As I crafted my online persona, I ticked all the boxes: female, nearby, and intriguing enough to catch his eye. It's not the size of the magnifying glass, just sheer determination and equal parts of cunning and humour.

> No frills, no fancy gadgets, just me, a keyboard and the pursuit of the truth.

24

BABOOSHKA
KATE BUSH

The Dark One - Part 2

MY INITIAL BAIT? A sassy blonde bombshell of an estate agent aged thirty-eight. More than a sprinkle younger than him. Her profile pic was all confidence, lounging in a jacuzzi with her squad, clearly living her best life. She was sharing a flat with her older brother, both parents deceased, no children, no ties, and fresh to the dating scene.

Knowing he was easily swayed by a pretty face, I knew this persona had potential, and boy, was I spot on. A mere "hello" was all it took to reel him in. He was on the hook faster than a fish at feeding time.

Despite my pounding heart and sinking disappointment, I slipped seamlessly into my alter ego. With the finesse of a seasoned actress, I masked my true intentions while extracting vital information from him, all while keeping up the charade.

I crafted her profile as the picture of contentment: thriving in a job she loved, settled in the area and on the lookout for love. She was looking for a supportive partner with an established career, someone who was secure and stable, and ideally, not already married.

His circumstances, however, were stated with a casual wave of the hand. An estranged wife residing overseas and now on a separate life path. It seems I had been cast away like a pair of last season's shoes. His conversation oozed with a youthful spirit, the kind that refuses to act his age.

He painted himself as a free spirit living solo, buoyed by a fulfilling career and grown, independent children who needed no more than a birthday card, and the occasional Christmas visit. He was eager to find a new love, someone to share life's adventures with, whatever those might be when you're juggling relationships like a circus clown, and was even open to the idea of having more children. Imagine that!

Sensing the hook was set, I suggested we meet, and he responded with the enthusiasm of a man who thought he'd bought the winning lottery ticket. He agreed, sealing a date for the following evening at a local bar.

To sweeten the deal, I sent a quick lunchtime message the next day complimenting him on our initial chat, though I "innocently" mentioned that I had forgotten to request a photo. After all, it would be a bit awkward to accidentally flirt with the bartender. He quickly responded, apologising profusely for the oversight, and promised to send one right away. And just like that, a minute later, there it was - the initial proof that I needed.

I imagined he expected an eager response, perhaps a flattering compliment, as the cherry on top. But there I was, caught in the surreal moment of receiving my own husband's dating photo in my inbox, while he remained blissfully unaware that it was his wife who had been reeling him in.

> Time for a little power play – cue radio silence.

Tick-tock. I decided to leave the pic on simmer, just to let the anticipation stew a bit.

Two hours later, as predicted, a simple question mark zipped across my screen, a digital nudge demanding attention.

It was time to deliver the bad news. I drafted my response with all the detached politeness I could muster, channelling the classic "Dear John" style, only I had to throw in a little extra sting with the dismissal.

> "Dear John,
>
> Having had time to think and not wanting to act hastily after just one quick chat, I've naturally shared my plans to meet you with my brother. He feels caution is required given your photo suggests that you may be an edge too old for me. Unfortunately, I won't be available this evening, but good luck with your search."

It didn't take long for another photo to barge into my inbox – this time of the self-proclaimed Adonis, wading in a lake, missing just enough clothing to make me wish he hadn't. His message oozed with bravado;

"I hope your brother one day looks like me at my age."

His feeble attempt at reasserting his masculinity only highlighted how distorted his self-image truly was.

Jason Momoa, he was not.

I replied with a heartfelt "Sorry, you seem like a nice guy etc."

Just enough for me to get blocked. Mission accomplished.

Cue the real me, the written-off wife, sending a text. I hadn't slept well, but I needed to interject and survey the carnage.

His response was low key, as expected. He'd been working and was tired. I responded with my usual level of support, advising a good night's sleep and casually boasted of my plans for that day – a trip to a leisure park with my girls.

As hard as it was to confront the reality, I had decided I would balance any newfound knowledge with healthy plans for me and mine. I knew I'd be nursing a heavy heart and my mind buzzing with the decision I'd made. I had to metal-up for the information that would be coming at me thick and fast in pursuit of the facts. Maintaining my mental health was paramount, and I knew I had a fight going forward, but the truth had to come out, it was the only way my head would, overtime, rule my heart.

Time to set up a new dating profile.

STEP FORWARD: A slim, sporty brunette in her early forties with a passion for photography. The kind of woman who might spend her weekends capturing the perfect sunrise or basking in the glory of nature, exactly the sort of adventurous spirit I knew, would pique his interest in another episode of digital romance.

He had previously remarked how he craved a hobby and maybe photography might just be the ticket. So, like a dutiful (and unsuspecting wife), I'd gifted him a high-end camera, complete with all the bells and whistles, for his birthday. He'd joined an evening class to "develop his skills." In hindsight, considering the class was predominantly female, I wasn't entirely sure what he was focusing on. My life has always been a tapestry of hobbies. Skiing, swimming and, most importantly, netball.

It seemed my sporty influence had rubbed off on him, or at least that's what he wanted me to think. He'd even bought himself a pair of football boots and proudly reported that he'd joined a club for footy practice. However, training was regularly "cancelled", and I don't recall there ever being a match. In reality, I doubt those boots ever saw the light of day outside their box. The ski lessons he had acquired previously were "free gratis" from a "female friend" working in one of the resorts. Go figure!

When you're dealing with a compulsive liar, curiosity quickly turns into paranoia. Every word, every story becomes suspect, and you're left questioning everything. You are continually being manipulated, but once the penny drops, the rose-tinted spectacles are replaced with magnifying glasses and absolute clarity.

But, back to my Scotland Yard operation.

My new alias was an artsy, outdoorsy type, who, when not teaching at university, spent her free time chasing sunrises and sunsets, ready to capture anything that might add a touch of magic to her portfolio. She was an adventure seeker with a Zen-like spirituality, looking for someone to share her journeys with. I probably should've added fishing to her list of hobbies, because sure enough, unsuspecting Romeo was reeled in with little effort. I figured this persona could dig a little deeper into his psyche, drawing out more of his thoughts on relationships and maybe asking him more about me. I painted a picture of what this teacher was looking for.

Her soulmate, her other half of a power couple, ideally DINKs – Double income. No kids. Throw in a dash of mutual respect, a sprinkle of shared goals, and all the other essentials for a balanced healthy relationship, and voila, you've got a dream team.

Laying it on the table seemed to draw him in, right into a false sense of security, that is.

I could almost feel the spark from his texts as he pictured himself as my forever guy. After all, his kids were grown and long gone, which meant he was free to mould himself into the perfect fit for my requirements, or at least, he would give it his best shot.

Enquiring about his status of being single, he confidently declared he was separated and already living his best life. Divorce? Just a formality, something he hadn't quite gotten around to yet but would, eventually.

I decided to go in with the ultimate icebreaker – I asked if he still loved his wife. His reply?

> "I did, but not anymore."

Cue the dramatic pause for effect. If I hadn't been living this surreal experience, I might've applauded the performance. But as it stood, I was too busy balancing the irony of the situation – crafting elaborate lies of my own to catch him in his.

His go-to excuse for our marriage crumbling was, "Long distance relationships just don't work".

A comforting notion, no doubt, for anyone in the military with a spouse and kids back home. I had to admire how he could make you feel you were the sun around which his entire universe evolved, then throw you under the bus. Little did he know he would experience a similar fate within twenty-four hours.

Feigning urgency, I spun some nonsense about my mum ringing on the phone, but assured him that I was eager to continue our chat. I matched his enthusiasm like a pro. Gushing about how lovely it was to finally talk to someone who listened. Naturally, he mirrored my sentiments, claiming he felt like he'd known me forever (too right you have)

This guy had it all – charm, wit, and a spectacularly stunning lack of awareness.

25

BEAUTIFUL LIAR
BEYONCE, SHAKIRA

THE NEXT MORNING, he woke up to a sweet little message in his inbox:

> "I was so impressed with your honesty and warm vibe last night that I even mentioned you to my mum." (The imaginary mum, of course) I playfully added, "She was giggling at the fact I don't have a photo of you yet, could you be a sweetheart and send one?"

> "Oh, and how are you fixed for a camera shoot after work around 5.15 pm? I know the perfect beach spot to catch the best images at sunset. We could even have a cheeky glass of vino as the sun goes down."

Within the hour, his pic arrived, and a request for the sat-nav details. This guy was so on the ball that I began to wonder if juggling a busy harem could be his true calling.

With another photo now in my possession and on simmer, I — his wife — figured it was the perfect moment to check in, you know, just to see how he was getting on. Asking the questions and hearing the lies first-hand was like a twisted little pep talk for myself, a necessary reinforcement to gear up for the next dose of reality I was about to rain down upon him.

I braced myself as I dialled, knowing I would soon hear that infuriatingly cheerful voice of his. When he was in these heady stages of a possible romance, his chat flowed with that happy, sing-song lilt, especially when the conversation was about him. He would even make a huge effort to ask how I was and how the girls were, an obvious smokescreen to mask his ill intention.

I pretended to be busy yet neutral, so my day never outshone his in the importance stakes.

He casually mentioned that he was feeling inspired and planned to hit the beach, camera in hand, to catch the sunset. When I asked if he was meeting up with other photographers, he quickly assured me, he was going solo.

"Oh, that sounds fabulous!" I chirped, masking my sarcasm with a thick layer of fake enthusiasm. "I can't wait to see what you capture!" How easily the lies rolled off his tongue. He probably had visions of a romantic sunset dalliance with the sporty Zen brunette, rolling in the sand. And I, the clueless wife, would naively buy every word.

We wrapped up the call with the usual pleasantries, but as I hung up, I knew the sun was about to set on his latest charade, another soft punch was on its way to him.

Within minutes of hanging up, he was already scrambling to lock down the date with Zen Girl.

A message popped up on my screen, breezy and confident: "Hi beautiful, has my pic come through?"

> I could feel the smugness radiating through the phone.

He must have thought he had this one in the bag, probably worried the only delay was she was still teaching in Uni or something equally as innocent. Little did he know, Zen girl had taken one look at the picture and promptly filed it under "Not as advertised."

Unfortunately for him, this well-heeled girl who had a critical eye for detail had decided his profile description was at war with the image she received.

You see, Zen Girl was expecting an athletic silver fox with a dashing sprinkle of salt & pepper hair, someone who embodied the "fit and fabulous at fifty" vibe. Instead, she got a bloke in a work polo shirt, sporting hair so white it could've deflected a nuclear blast. And don't get me started on that gut. Let's just say, it wasn't the six-pack he'd hinted at. More of a keg.

At 4 pm sharp, Zen girl finally replied. Just leaving work.

> "Yes, I got your pic. I've been mulling it over all day, but I'm just not feeling it. You've marked the salt & pepper option on hair colour with no trace of pepper in the image sent. Maybe you should have simply gone with "white". I have no desire to start anything when you aren't being honest."

Now as the dutiful wife who usually worked my hair colouring magic to tone down his stark white to something more, shall we say, steely and edgy, I knew this comment would hit him where it hurt.

The power of a good toner is not to be underestimated, and without it, he was looking more Gandalf than George Clooney.

With no witty comeback, no defence, he simply skulked off with his half-truths and outright fabrications.

And just like that, the Zen Girl got blocked.

And as for those sunset pics? They never materialised – just some mumbled excuse about how the sun was setting too quickly and him and being at the wrong vista to capture it.

ONE WEEK LATER...

Enter the nurse. Not just any nurse, mind you. Held in high esteem for her dedication and compassion, she was a walking recruitment ad for Healthcare, New Zealand. Who could resist the allure of such a magnetic personality?

She sported curly brown hair, threaded with golden highlights that caught the sun just right. She was the kind of woman who loved to walk her dog morning and evening, the kind of routine that made her seem grounded, and dependable – just the right mix of earthy and wholesome.

Her eyes, though, those twinkling eyes, could draw anyone in, a sparkling combination of warmth and mischief. She had that perfect blend of humour and sensibility, the type that could make you laugh at your own misery while simultaneously handing you a tissue. Perfect for him, obviously, and another opportunity not to miss, as he responded to her reach out text.

A young family member of his had just been hospitalised for tests. His schedule was already bursting at the seams with work, hospital visits, and the occasional acknowledgement of my existence. What better to throw in than a caring Nurse to soothe his self-serving soul? "Unleash her!"

The timing was impeccable, like the universe had handed me a golden opportunity to test his loyalty yet again. As the orchestrator of the unfolding drama, I held the strings, manipulating the plans to suit my goals.

After all, everyone deserves three strikes before they're out, right?

Our nurse, by the way, was conveniently closer to his age, loved the great outdoors, adored 80s music (because who doesn't), and was a whizz at cooking outdoor feasts for her family at weekends. Oh, and you wouldn't know it, she lived just across the bay, practically spitting distance, accessible. You couldn't have scripted it better if you tried.

My success in luring him in with these various personas had turned me into a one-woman show, flipping between characters like a Mrs Doubtfire sketch running between food, dining courses, and facemasks, minus the face cream.

Our daily dialogues unfolded.

By day I was the concerned English wife, checking in to see how he was coping. By night, I was the compassionate nurse, lending a sympathetic ear while he dutifully reported from the hospital bedside. And boy, did he milk it.

Leaning into the nurse's empathy, he painted the picture of the doting family man, providing heartfelt updates on the patient's progress with the kind of sincerity that made me believe it myself. Almost.

On the other hand, his updates to me, the wife, were lacklustre. I sensed in his tone that there were other places he would rather be. Like anywhere that wasn't filled with the smell of antiseptic and bleeping monitors. Routine visits to the ward were a chore, and I got the two versions of him, both where he simply pretended to care.

Then came the little gem of fun that made all the effort worthwhile. I didn't realise it at the time, but it would factor in later, just when I needed it to.

While the nurse enquired about the name of the patient, his clumsy thumbs, aided by the wonders of predictive text, birthed the name

> "Cucumber,"

instead of the intended name. We both burst out laughing. Yes, emojis were involved, as he quickly apologised. I insisted it was such a cute, endearing name and so "Cucumber" stuck, becoming our little inside joke between him and his imaginary nurse. Little did I know that this amusing slip would play a starring role in the final act of our marriage.

Meanwhile, I — the estranged wife — quietly slid further into the background, edging ever closer to the inevitable discard. It was a strange irony. My words, my characters, kept drawing him in, like moths to a flame. I seemed to be his ideal woman, in every possible variation, even as I was quietly writing myself out of the script.

His attention, of course, has wandered to someone else, naturally across the bay. But "go me" that "someone else" was as real as a unicorn doing Pilates. The woman was fictional, just a figment of his imagination, and yet, here he was having full-blown flirty exchanges with her. Classic. We even joked about how after a gruelling long shift, as the nurse, I'd dozed off in my imaginary hot tub, only to wake up to the smell of my dinner cremating itself on the barbecue. And in true, "knight in shining delusion armour" fashion, he assured me that had he spotted the smoke signals, a swim across the bay to save the day would have been in order.

Meanwhile, he had his hands full hosting "Cucumber", his convalescing guest who would now be camping out with him for a few weeks. He was available to meet whenever I was free, and once "Cucumber" was tucked up for the night, no doubt. Our chats had only been casual and brief to this point. My photo was visible on my profile. Sensing an opportunity, I chose not to ask for a photo of him, instead probing a little deeper into his living arrangements. It was time to subtly assess his intentions.

I dropped the ol' homeowner bomb. Seventeen years settled, no intention of moving, family living nearby. His response? Polished and as smooth as I expected. Area manager of a national company travelling all over for work, he explained, and his current home was merely a temporary sanctuary, leased until the dust from his divorce settled. Oh, and he also adored the bay area as a prime place for him to live. With his offspring living independently, he was happy to stay in the locale. He had a remarkable knack for fitting seamlessly with anyone's brief.

The tempo of our conversation picked up, no doubt because I hadn't demanded a photo yet. I thought it best to stay away from that approach. He was free that evening and keen to make the pilgrimage across the bay. He offered to bring food and drinks for a cook-up on the Barbecue that evening, swimming togs at the ready for a dip in the hot tub afterwards (of course, he was).

By this time, I'd gathered enough intel to write a novella. His "temporary" home? A storm shelter, waiting for the divorce weather to clear. Why the wait? Was he hoping for some reverse dowry, perhaps? The marriage had barely lifted off the runway, so I wasn't sure what loot he thought was waiting in the wings.

I, on the other hand, had built equity in terms of a home, owned a car and had a career that was real, not between fantasy and reality. So, what were his true intentions? The man had perfected the art of bunny-hopping between countries and lives, bringing with him highs and lows, and a suitcase full of excuses.

By now, I believe I had heard and done enough.

I had the "tea" on him. This gave me a lot to think about, and once again, my wrath was on its way to him.

26

TITANIUM

SIA | DAVID GUETTA

I FELT it was time to give him the news and bring this final dating chapter to a close. A deliberate pause followed as the nurse weighed her response.

 "Dear John,

> You seem nice, but I was hoping for someone with more security and ambition."

Within 30 minutes, a simple "No worries" marked the end of this digital dalliance. A final blow to his inflated — fragile — ego. But what more could you expect from a man driven by instant gratification and hollow affection?

JOB DONE. CASE CLOSED

It felt bittersweet, yet justified, delivering this parting shot as the final flourish of my little "revealing" side project. A precise reminder, perfectly aimed, to let him know that his baby-blue eyes and slick charm weren't the universal currency he thought they were. Certainly not in my world.

And definitely not with the women of the calibre I'd created—strong, sharp, and built to see straight through his brand of flimsy persuasion. It felt like a poetic justice to pull this off not once, not twice, but three times. Foolproof. Seamless. A triple triumph against the likes of him. By the end, it wasn't just a win—it was art.

He no longer felt like a husband but a case study. His human behaviour resembled a robotic entity. Early on I fell for his charm and practical capabilities, yet beneath the surface, he remained mechanical and detached. I accomplished my mission.

Although I had the satisfaction of unmasking his true nature and bringing him down a notch or three, I knew there would be no winners in this precarious game.

IN THREE DAYS, I would be collecting him from the airport. What then?

Did he have an end game? Could he truly sustain this charade indefinitely?

I visualised him as a comedy character running around the earth, hastily crafting new identities every ten minutes. He considered himself the ultimate Casanova in his own Walter Mitty Syndrome-afflicted imagination. His dreams were of dalliance, regardless of the discord he would create. Me, Myself, and I was his motto.

Realising the futility of engaging further in this charade, I understood that disconnecting from his existence would demand all my inner calm and unwavering focus. After all, he knew nothing of my findings and would still assume the gravitational pull on the strings of my heart.

It was time to reclaim my peace of mind and leave behind the relentless cycle of uncertainty he brought to my life.

Chatting with hairdressing clients and friends over the years has given me insight into closure. The distress and confusion are repeatedly experienced when dealing with situations and relationships that have no genuine sense of closure. It's heart-wrenching to witness their struggles as they grapple with unanswered questions and hidden truths. The what ifs. The how could I's.

Meanwhile, I found myself in a unique position with a bird's-eye view of my situation. While it felt like a strange privilege to possess such knowledge, it also weighed me down.

Uncovering the truth firsthand demanded a significant amount of emotional energy, leaving me constantly drained yet oddly grateful for the clarity it provided.

> In hindsight, I had fallen victim to his charm and manipulation, mistaking his "love bombing" for genuine affection.

But now, with newfound clarity, I saw him for what he truly was. A cunning predator disguised as a hopeless romantic, ready to sink his teeth into anyone naïve enough to trust him.

Each day, I found myself maintaining a façade with The Dark One, through our sombre gritty drama. I engaged in conversations about his upcoming visit and our plans for the calendar. He had volunteered to do some decorating whilst I was at work. However, amidst these discussions, I couldn't help but carry the weight of my sister's impending operation, a priority that consumed my thoughts.

While I didn't indulge in deep conversations about the future, I held onto the belief that further revelations and even more clarity would be exposed as events unfolded. I needed to witness the web of lies that he had always shrouded our marriage with. His dialogue was going to be interesting, to say the least.

Waiting at the airport in our usual spot, the time ticking by I began checking my watch repeatedly. Wondering if there had been a delay of some sort. I hadn't heard a peep from him throughout the entire journey. So, I did what any sane person would do. I interrogated the airline staff who confirmed he was indeed on the passenger list. Great, but where was he physically? He wasn't answering my calls, and I even tried the dark alleys of social media, all to no avail. Time was ticking, and I had my girls to pick up from school. Priorities, you know?

Upon returning home, I received a message from his friend who conveniently owned a business a stone's throw away. Lo-and-behold, there he had arrived, like a misplaced parcel in transit. Turned out he had taken a detour and ended up at a different pickup point – because why stick to the plan when you can jazz it up with a dash of chaos?

Of course, his lack of communication during the journey was blamed on wonky Wi-Fi, as if Wi-Fi was ever known for its reliability. Classic.

But the kicker? He was fuming on the phone call. I was accused of being the neglectful wife who failed to materialise at the airport. As if I had the time or inclination to pull off such a stunt. Three weeks prior, we entertained the idea of a collection point at a petrol garage's short-stay parking lot.

A fleeting notion, contingent on impeccable timing and a lack of flight delays. Yet, without a whisper of discussion before or during his transcontinental journey, that's where he found himself stranded. He couldn't fathom that a simple conversation could have spared us this debacle, instead, he chose to deflect his embarrassment by pinning it on me.

After all, accountability wasn't his strong suit and shifting blame was as effortless as breathing. But.

Alas, I couldn't help but chuckle at the sheer audacity of this man. Because, in his world, building castles in the air and mistaking them for reality is just another Tuesday.

So, with a silent eye-roll, I hauled myself back out to retrieve him. The car journey home was like a rolling stalemate. But hey, the new enlightened me had become a pro at plastering a smile on my face when needed.

Arriving back at his home away from home, through thinly veiled tension and the reunion with my girls as the family ambassadors, he had no choice but to don his grown-up hat and blend in.

But who was I kidding? His mind was still elsewhere, still stewing over the pricey cab fare due to the airport fiasco.

On top of this, he was back on the cigarettes. Previously his passion to give them up led him to a cessation group, and I had been his faithful supporter in his quest to quit smoking.

As if on cue, at the first sign of stress, he had relapsed. It's like riding a bike, isn't it?

Except, you know, with more coughing than pedalling.

Now as I watched him puff away like a chimney, I couldn't help but feel, well, past caring. His dishevelled look was amplified by the need for a haircut.

It's a strange dance. Being privy to the intricate and deceptive details of my partner's hushed secrets, and now having him standing in front of me, everything was different.

Life had taken a darkly comedic turn. As he droned on, his words became little more than meaningless noise to me. My imagination wandered into a bizarre scenario: if I were to cut off his head, would it simply roll across the floor, finally silencing him for good? Or would the lies keep spilling out, defying the absence of lungs and vocal cords?

The casual conversation continued with me effortlessly slipping into the role of a friendly jailer. I clicked away on my phone, alternating between idle chatter with him and checking in on my sister – who was bravely facing down her battle with cancer. As her operation drew near, she knew nothing of my situation. From my perspective, her battle with cancer eclipsed my murky path, relegating my struggles to the back burner.

He, on the other hand, thrived on adoration, so depriving him of the spotlight wasn't going to be easy. My plate would be overflowing the next few days with hospital visits, so as planned, we headed off to pick up paint to decorate the kitchen, a convenient distraction to occupy him which I hoped would keep him off my scent for a while.

> Back home, I opened some wine to numb my skull and at the same time amplify a joyful demeanour.

I knew intimate relations were going to be begrudgingly had, and this was the best way for me to disassociate.

Maintaining the façade was crucial; every interaction and reaction served as a valuable insight into his true character. It was part of the puzzle I had partially solved and was determined to decipher fully. Besides, with my packed schedule that week, it would be all too easy to keep him at arm's length. I knew divorce loomed on the horizon, and I was determined to navigate it on my terms, armed with the evidence I needed to sever ties. This evening would be the last time he would own me in this way. I would lay back and think of England.

The next morning, I was up early. With a sigh and a steaming cup of coffee, I braced myself for a busy day of mobile hairdressing. While I would normally book a couple of days off to cater to his arrival, life had other plans, my loyal clients awaiting their turn in my diary, and of course, hospital visits now included in my busy schedule.

He waved me off. He had his grand decorating plans to keep him occupied in my absence. We would normally have some text exchanges and progress reports throughout the day, but I was so busy, and he assured me he had plenty to do ensuring a productive day.

I returned home from work later that day, half expecting to find a transformed living space worthy of a magazine spread. Instead, I was greeted by the sight of one small patch of ceiling receiving a makeover.

Suppressing the urge to critique his efforts, I plastered on a smile and casually inquired about the number of coats applied. Two coats? One can only hope.

His nod with little feedback demonstrated his dwindling enthusiasm for the task at hand and a reminder of the reality unfolding around us.

With my girls spending the night at their father's, I decided to treat us to an indulgent takeaway, which lifted his spirits at the prospect of being catered to and I played the role of his gracious hostess.

Beneath the surface, I was grappling with a sense of inner conflict, torn between the obligation to placate him and the unwavering loyalty I felt towards my sister's plight.

Alas, events would unfold sooner than anticipated.

After our Indian feast, accompanied by a liquid libation or two, we migrated from the table to the sofa ready to engage in some post-dinner banter. As the food and drinks worked their magic, he seemed to loosen up a tad like a rusty hinge yielding to a bit of WD-40.

We exchanged pleasantries about our day, mine a buzzing hive of hairdressing activity, with clients wishing my sister well.... His day? – well, that remained a mystery only solvable by Sherlock Holmes himself.

His day seemed to resemble a slow-motion replay of a snail's journey. Lots of effort but minimal progress. I gently probed about his day, but my sympathetic enquiry was met with the inevitable dance of deception. Predictably, his responses resembled a carefully crafted work of fiction, but I played along, eager to see how far down the rabbit hole he would go. And true to form, he didn't disappoint. Phone calls to family, and friends ringing to make plans, and he needed a little siesta. I assured him there was no rush with the paint job and it was nice that he was willing to pitch in.

I sensed his sudden realisation that he was providing a service to me didn't sit well with him. He was doing me a favour and I dared to question him…. Imparting to me how he utilised his time seemed to chafe against his sense of entitlement.

Overpromising on the decorating and underdelivering I believe was intended to provoke a reaction to create an argument.

But – I wasn't biting!

27

CRY ME OUT
PIXI LOTT

The Dark One - Part 3

IF HE SENSED a change in me beyond my sister's cancer, he did display some distortion and distance, like a defence mechanism. I was too calm, not playful to his tune. This didn't resonate with him. He needed total compliance, and I was confusing him.

Experience with him over time taught me that the transition from a normal conversation to a meltdown could happen at any time and arrive from nowhere – like a surprise party! I recognised now that this was one of those "special" moments. I could feel his dissatisfaction bubbling and his brain scheming for my downfall. His intention was to knock me down a peg or two and safely reclaim his throne.

With just the two of us present, his ineptitude knew no bounds as he leapt off the sofa like a caffeinated kangaroo and headed towards the patio doors, arms flailing, and a voice booming like a one-man opera.

"Here you go again!"

"What's wrong now?" I replied with a dry wit, preparing for the inevitable onslaught of absurdity.

Just another classic dance of dysfunction, I thought. I remained seated, unruffled by his theatrics. Historically, the old 'me' would have been an eager participant to chase and fix things. As he peered through the glass window, expecting the usual panicked response, he lit a cigarette, his head shaking in a comical blend of animation and disdain.

After a five-minute cooldown period, he finally paced back into the room. I was still sitting firmly on the sofa, unmoved and opting for a 'wait and see' approach. A personal favourite in dealing with emotional tantrums.

But lo-and-behold, he resurfaced with another argument, armed with complaints about being abandoned at the airport. My failure to wait indefinitely for his majestic return was the ultimate betrayal. I calmly pointed out that mind-reading wasn't among my many talents, and the blame squarely rested on his shoulders for failing to communicate.

Of course, he couldn't help tossing in a few bonus accusations, claiming I didn't want him there. I hadn't texted him from work that day, yada, yada, yada. I rolled my eyes so hard I thought I sprained an optic nerve. I reiterated that his conspiracy theories were pure fiction and urged him to stop treating them like gospel truth. Naturally, he continued to twist the conversation, but he was ill-equipped. I was ready for him.

Realising his attempt to browbeat me had failed, he begrudgingly backed down. Clearing the table, I reminded him of my sister's impending operation and suggested we call it a night, we were both exhausted. With the absence of empathy for anyone but yours truly, he visibly displayed as restless and agitated within my walls and territory.

As he stepped outside for a final smoke break, I took a moment of solitude, relishing the brief reprieve from our shared space.

Flashbacks of his digital dating dalliances fed into my negative thoughts. I had to bite my tongue. I didn't need any more eruptions that day.

The food and wine served as a perfect sedative, with a good night's sleep as my main objective, I dove into bed eager to put the day behind us.

I rose the next morning, calm and organised, serving a hearty English breakfast armed with my frying pan and a side of diplomacy. I had turned the page on yesterday's melodrama.

My schedule was clear: hospital duty awaited me around 1.30 pm, a bustling ninety-minutes drive away. Meanwhile, he would tackle the decorating and the school run, collecting the girls at 3.30 pm. With breakfast sorted, he took himself off for a shower. Shortly after, I heard him shout a message of thanks as he appeared at the top of the stairs holding some motorcycle gear.

I had briefly forgotten about this gift purchased for him on a limited-stock deal. It was after he had absconded the country previously, but before my "awakening" of his infidelity. Away from plain sight, they had been stashed away. It certainly wasn't high on my priority to offer them to him, given my recent updated knowledge. But he clearly remembered my mention of them and being a scavenger of gifts, he had stumbled across them in the spare room.

He was thrilled with the two pairs of motorcycle trousers that fitted perfectly. His mood skyrocketed as he beckoned me to join in and admire his newfound treasures. For a brief, shining moment, I basked in his glow of approval. Though watching him marvel at himself in the mirror, I couldn't help but stifle a laugh at the absurdity of it all.

Here he was revelling in gear meant for a non-existent motorcycle. But no doubt, he would procure one somehow. I received another smile of approval as he pulled on the gloves to complete the ensemble...... until they didn't fit... Cue the look of disappointment, complete with attempts to force them onto his hands as if sheer willpower alone could stretch the fabric. "They're too tight!" he exclaimed, his face a mixture of determination and dismay. And all I could think of was, "What, like you?"

Fiddling with the wrist straps asking if we could go and exchange them, I delivered the harsh truth: limited stock and the outdated receipt meant that we were stuck with them. "Other stores might have some!" he pouted as his temporary wave of adoration for me subsided.

My mind wandered back to his previous visit, involving his impulsive purchase of a car he had to have, a much bigger spend. With little research on the overall cost of running this vehicle, it subsequently needed more investment to be roadworthy resulting in buyer's remorse. That car now sat in his friend's garage business needing repair.

Yet here he was now, sulking over some ill-fitting gloves. As I could offer no immediate solution, he tossed them aside stating, what a shame and I should have saved my money. I had been striving to uphold a façade of civility, but we were only three days in, and I was on the brink of losing my composure.

As I reminded him of my sister's current situation – an ongoing illness with an outcome still hanging in the balance – the other Liz in my head made her grand entrance.

You know her – the Love Accountant. The one with a pencil skirt, glasses perched on her nose, flipping through emotional spreadsheets, thinking things like: *"This bloke's already in arrears."*

With impeccable timing and zero tolerance for nonsense, I stepped up and hit the delete button on this drama.

I rested my gaze squarely on him, leaned in ever so slightly and enquired,

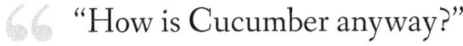 "How is Cucumber anyway?"

The look of alarm and confusion that washed over him as he scrambled to invent an answer was priceless. His plaid face twitched, and for a glorious moment, he didn't know whether to apologise or run for cover. His brain appeared to recognise the word but struggled to register how it fitted into our circumstance. As I waited patiently for a response, I raised an eyebrow to add a touch of sarcasm. His mumbled "yeah, okay, who, err", only highlighted his inability to string together coherent thoughts. It was like witnessing someone afflicted with sudden onset amnesia, unable to recall even the simplest details. It was the first glimmer of satisfaction I had felt after two years of being kept in the dark by this shapeshifter. I had caught him off guard, his mind now racing to reconcile how I could know about a part of his life he had kept hidden from me.

He was busted but he was unclear to what extent. He was under attack, and I could practically see the gears turning in his head as he tried to spin this in his favour. As I gathered my things to leave, his desperation was palpable. He muttered and bickered, trying to find the words to give me some kind of ultimatum. "Are you going to be like this or are we going to sort this out?" he demanded, seeking a definitive answer. His realisation that I had uncovered his web of deceit left him seething with rage, yet he couldn't quite grasp how I had managed it.

I remained unfazed, offering only a calm assurance that we could discuss it further when I returned later. In the meantime, I suggested he carry on with the decorating and reminded him to do the school run. My whole focus was to get on the road and see my sister.

I knew there would be little introspection on his part, but the cat was out of the bag at least.

Driving through the chaotic traffic, my mind wandered to our recent confrontation. Partially exposing him and then leaving him in a state of uncertainty was never going to work in my favour. As I finally found a parking spot near the ward, I received a message from him instructing me to check my email. Odd timing, considering he knew I was on a hospital visit. I checked my inbox, only to find it empty as I proceeded to the ward. Frustrated, I replied, questioning the urgency of this message, especially given the circumstances.

Arriving at the ward, another text arrived stating I needed to check the elusive email. Visiting time was due to start so I dashed outside to search for a stronger signal. Indeed, the email was now there, only to be met with his angry words declaring his dramatic departure from the house because of my supposed unwillingness to compromise, basically, I wouldn't cater to his demands. He was leaving.

My immediate concern was the safety of my girls, left uncollected from school. My enquiry on this via a text to him was met with silence.

Returning to the hospital ward, I navigated my way to my sister's bedside where I found comfort in her cheerful demeanour, despite the grogginess from anaesthesia. Our conversation with regard to a successful outcome of her operation buoyed my spirits. That's all I needed to hear. I was overwhelmed with relief for her, yet my mind raced with worry as I had no time to make alternative arrangements for my girls to be picked up from school. His abrupt exit left me with no option but to leave my sister and race back down the motorway to home. She was very gracious in my excuses to head off early due to traffic, and with a hug and a heavy heart, I swiftly located my car and made haste. Driving home, it was abundantly clear he was selfish, reckless and utterly devoid of concern for anyone but himself.

It's not that I didn't already know this, but having to leave my sister and in turn my girls left in the lurch, it wasn't like a penny dropped. It felt like an emotional tsunami of this man's selfish indifference bearing down on me.

28

GOLD DUST WOMAN
STEVIE NICKS

ARRIVING at school just in the nick of time, I was relieved to see my girls in their usual happy stance, a welcome respite from the inner panic I was experiencing. As they asked about his whereabouts, I offered a vague explanation, shielding them from the reality of his departure. I updated them on good news about their aunty which pleased them both followed by the usual chatter about what we would be having for dinner.

On entering our house, I scanned the scene for any trace of him. I climbed the stairs to the spare room where his things were generally stored. His suitcase was gone, as was the motorcycle gear, packaging left on the floor – except for a lone pair of biker gloves.

> It was as if a malevolent spirit had been exorcised from our home leaving behind a lingering sense of relief.

I wasn't too surprised. After all, some problems are a bit too real for a serial escapist like him to handle. And that's when it hit me.

This ridiculous, vegetable-themed blunder was exactly what I needed. It was as if the universe had handed me a cosmic gift, wrapped in green skin and good timing.

Little did I know, "Cucumber" would be the plot twist in this whole saga, delivering more than just a giggle, but the clarity I didn't know I needed. Honestly, it was the least I could wish for. Thank you, Cucumber, for giving me the last laugh.

The next day was spent ridding the house of any superficial belongings he may have left behind. As I was tidying around, I noticed a curious disappearance: my daughter's Samsung tablet had vanished from its usual spot on the kitchen table and now there was only one, which belonged to her younger sister.

His capacity for mischief knew no bounds, but stooping to stealing from a child? That's a new low, even for him. My attempts to coax a response from him via text were met with silence. As I pondered his whereabouts, a casual stroll through Facebook revealed a detour to Spain, so I resorted to contacting his mother, who in a display of parental apathy, promised to relay my message but showed little concern for his transgressions.

Predictably, this purged a fiery retort from him, annoyed he had been exposed for pilfering from a child. He offered to return the tablet via a rendezvous at the airport in two weeks. Suffice it to say, I had no intention of engaging with him any further and decided to spare myself the headache and wait for the postman to do his thing.

And as if that weren't enough, I later realised the soundbar for my telly had decided to join in on the disappearing act. He had truly filled his boots, but at least the tablet emerged three weeks later back into the hands of its rightful owner.

Months passed and as the dust settled, I began initiating the divorce proceedings. Initially, he seemed cooperative via email, but upon receiving the paperwork, his tone shifted dramatically. Suddenly he was playing the victim card and highlighting me as a person who was biased against him.

I kept the allegations to a minimum with no mention of infidelity, but he refuted my version and stated his position that – he would be filing his divorce petition the following year.

> Bless his heart, he clearly hadn't grasped the concept that his signature was the only thing standing between me and freedom.

The legal wheels were set in motion as he had indeed made his mark in the appropriate box. In the end, the divorce was finalised bringing an end to the mercifully brief two years of this dark presence.

Throughout this time, I immersed myself in understanding the toll emotional stress can take, and how to navigate its aftermath. It became a mission to reclaim my sense of self from the web of manipulation and negativity that he seemed to weave effortlessly around us both.

I discovered online therapies and resources that became my lifelines, offering clarity and a pathway to healing. One of the most profound influences was Dr. Ramami Durvasala. Her wisdom became a daily guide, her videos an anchor.

She has a gift for unravelling the complexities of toxic personalities, laying bare their patterns, and explaining the "why" behind their behaviours. Her words felt like a mirror reflecting the truth I had come to know, a reminder that some people, instead of nurturing light, would rather set the entire room ablaze.

Being tethered to someone who thrives on emotional chaos is more than exhausting – it's neurologically disruptive. The rollercoaster of extreme highs and lows chips away at your stability, sending your amygdala into overdrive, and keeping your mind locked in a state of hypervigilance as if bracing for the next blow.

What is the amygdala you ask?

The amygdala is like your emotional command centre, a small, almond-shaped structure in the brain, responsible for processing feelings, memories, and responses to stress. When it's pushed too hard and for too long, it begins to misfire, leaving you perpetually on edge, like a doorbell that won't stop ringing.

The prolonged strain doesn't just live in your head – it seeps into your body, draining your reserves until adrenal fatigue sets in. That unshakeable exhaustion, the need for endless sleep yet never feeling rested, becomes a cycle you can't seem to break.

Dr Ramanis' teachings became my balm, her wisdom didn't just pull me out of the storm – it helped me rebuild. I owe much of my sanity and wellness to her, though she'll never know me personally, her words were a hand that reached through the darkness and steadied me. For that, I am endlessly grateful.

Relationships will always have their ups and downs and can conclude for many reasons. For some, the allure of maintaining a façade and preserving the comfort and familiarity outweigh the desire for truth. They cling to the stability of their home and family, hesitant to disrupt the status quo, especially for the sake of the children. Much of the time, it's about a house, and generally joint finances. Yet for me, living a life veiled in deception felt like a disservice – a life lived in shadows rather than the full light of truth.

And just when I thought I'd seen all there was to see with him, he hit me with one last little gem. It was that kind of moment that serves as a litmus test for how far you've come down the road of "enlightenment" or at the very least, "indifference."

So, there I was, packing for a trip and doing the usual suitcase audit when I came across his favourite travel companion: the well-worn suitcase that played third wheel between New Zealand and the UK on his little back-and-forth world tour.

As any battle-scarred traveller knows, you can't just grab a suitcase and go. You have to dig through the pockets for the inevitable – scrappy old receipts and the odd rogue sock. Anyway, as I reached into a pocket, felt a box, and thought, "What new horror is this?"

> And there it was: a bumper box of condoms.

A bold, unapologetic, symbol of his legacy, in thirty neatly wrapped pieces. It was like fate was dangling the ultimate punchline in front of me, daring me to lose it. But instead of sparking any rage or sorrow, I just burst out laughing.

This wasn't a grand revelation, just another gold-star reminder of who he really was. I felt nothing, no shock, no sting, no disappointment. It was just one of those rare moments of triumphant calm when you realise you've moved on.

As I bid farewell to this chapter in my life, I couldn't help but relish in the poetic justice of his downfall, a fitting end to his reign of deceit.

Or so I thought...... They say these types have a knack for reaching back into their past, in the attempt to reignite old flames. And true to form, it took seven years after I'd closed that particular chapter for him to resurface. One day, out of the blue, his name flashed across the top of my phone screen like a ghost I hadn't invited back. My eyes widened as an involuntary shiver ran down my spine. I had him blocked on all social media platforms – How was he even contacting me, and why?

Panic and fear got the better of me as I tapped on the notification, realising he'd found a loophole: my business page. Not only had he been lurking, liking my posts, and presumably scrolling through my life updates like some digital archaeologist, but he'd also sent a message: Three words:

> "How you doing?"

Before you ask - no, ladies, it didn't come with the charming Joey Tribbiani energy. There was no cheeky grin or lovable quirk behind it. It was more like a question delivered in the tone of someone flipping through their Rolodex of opportunities, hoping to find one that might still pick up the phone.

Spoiler Alert: it wasn't going to be me.

Marriage number four, eh? Must be losing its spark. I mean, nothing screams *"I'm used goods"*. Quite like a bloke recycling himself through a conveyor belt of brides... And worse still, his profile pic was a snap from – wait for it – his *most recent wedding day*. Classy. Could he stoop any lower? At this rate, he'd need a shovel.

With such an ongoing collection of wives who serve a temporary purpose, perhaps a guillotine would expedite matters – a swift chop to the marital ties if you will.

I was now living a new life in Australia, far from his romantic escapades. If I entertained his advances, he would have spun some yarn about visiting his kids, who *just so happened* to live near me. Perfect excuse for a rendezvous over coffee.

Translation: He would attempt to plant his flag in my territory. But let's not kid ourselves, when it comes to this guy, there's no second act, it's just the same tired script.... He's the guy at the party who's always trying to impress everyone with his tales of adventure and conquest, conveniently leaving out the part where he's crashing on someone else's couch.

But this isn't my first rodeo.

I saw through his thinly veiled attempt to cosy up to me whilst simultaneously plotting his escape from his current situation.

I realised his unsuspecting wife would be blissfully unaware of her husband's sneaky little digital reach out to an ex-wife. So, what did I do?

I left his sneaky little message hanging, unanswered and unacknowledged in the digital abyss. But not without snapping a screenshot first, for insurance purposes. Because the one thing I've learned, it's receipts that matter. Collect your receipts in all aspects of life, my friends.

Because in the Land Down Under, we don't just wrestle crocs, but sneaky snakes in the grass, too. Venomous ones, at that!

So, be on the lookout.

29

LONG AND WINDING ROAD
THE BEATLES

FORTY YEARS BEHIND THE CHAIR.

Where did the time go? It's like I've blinked, and here I am, still feeling like that sixteen-year-old holding her first pair of scissors with a gleam in her eye and a head full of ambition. I remember that thrill, that spark from that very first snip.

Hairstyles have come and gone, big perms, crimping and backcombing, even the odd rat-tail (may that one rest in peace) but the real key to being a great stylist is knowing the foundations. The techniques. Hand me a solid pair of scissors, a comb and a sectioning clip, and I'll make magic happen. Sure, we've got thinning scissors, razors, clippers, and every gadget under the sun, but it all boils down to how you wield them. I would always encourage trainees to be as bespoke as possible and learn first how hair moves so they know what to take from each section- and how to slice and create every part of the style with your scissors only. My training was rigorous. The clippers were only for cleaning the edges. You want to master a crew cut? You couldn't just buzz it all off in five minutes.

> You earned that cut, painstakingly, snipping away "scissor over comb" and all done by eye.

Hairdressing takes years to master, and that's no exaggeration. Three years to get the basics under your belt, then a few more to refine them, and after that? It's a lifelong apprenticeship. You're always updating and cramming the courses in to stay on trend.

Every head of hair teaches you something new, and working with different textures and growth patterns is the best crash course there is. You know what makes fine hair look limp, what makes thick hair stubborn, and how humidity can make hair throw a tantrum.

And transformations? They're the best. When someone walks in with hair down to their waist and says, "Chop it all off! – I'm not fazed." In fact, I live for it! If it's the right choice for them, I'm all in. There's nothing more satisfying than seeing someone walk out with that bounce like they're carrying an entirely new outlook, all because of a haircut.

People think it's the fancy updos or the Hollywood-esque blow outs that get us excited, but it's not just glamour styles; I've always found the most joy in solving people's styling issues or giving them something they didn't realise they could have. It can transform a person when you give them a different version of themselves.

Now I've had clients come to me after experiencing a bad hair day at the hands of someone who needed further training on their cutting techniques, and it's very satisfying to correct the issues the client has been struggling with.

But a good cut? I'll shout out to the stylist because I know what it took to get there. It's a mark of respect among hairdressers – you see the precision, the training, the passion in a good cut.

One of my golden rules? Always tell clients they can come back in for tweaks. Do you need the fringe a bit shorter? Give me a shout! It's the trust and openness that makes a client-stylist relationship last forty years – and counting. My English clients still come to me for advice and guidance on their hair – and everything else.

I must shout out to the barbers too. They have been behind the game with basic charging for many years even though the times have evolved, and overheads have soared. Gone are the days of a quick hack job. Today's barbers offer you an experience as if they're chiselling a Roman statue. In the last decade, they have finally caught up to the fact – they can't charge 1970s prices when they're handing out haircuts worthy of a red-carpet premiere.

With their shops looking like a scene from a magazine spread, they've nailed the art of edgy décor, neon lights, and shelves stacked with more grooming products than a Hollywood dressing room. You walk in and they practically hand you the key to the city – or at least a cold beer, which is almost as good. You're seated on a throne that's more supportive than most relationships, and then they wrap you up in a hot towel treatment that has you feeling reborn by the end. Within forty minutes, they can turn a Sunday morning scruff into a head-turner.

Working alongside De Angelo – a top-notch barber here in Oz – has been a lesson in more than just haircuts.

I learned they aren't just there to tidy up split ends; they're practically certified in giving men a place to sit down, unwind, unpack their thoughts and open up. Barbers are waking up to the true value they hold, realising they can send a man out of that chair feeling ten feet tall, ready to take on the world, or at the very least, their inbox.

These barbers pour their talent, their energy, and their spirit into transforming their clients from the inside out. Every stroke of the razor is calculated, and every towel is a wrap ritual. They're not just grooming hair, they're grooming a sense of dignity back into blokes.

And over in the corner, the Oz hairdressers stand watching with arms folded, trying not to look impressed as barbers work their magic. It's the art, the ease, the raw ability to shape a personality from a bit of facial fuzz. And we can't help but be slightly envious.

I can't walk past a top-notch fade without tipping my invisible hat. If I'm queued up behind a guy with a smooth fade, I'll tap him on the shoulder and mutter,

"Stick with your barber, mate, they're doing you justice." But if I see a botch job with chunky ledges you could abseil down, well, that's when my mouth stays zipped – but in my head, it's a rock concert. Led Zepplin's *"Stairway to Heaven."*

Though my hairdressing roots are firmly planted in England. I've been living in Brisbane since 2020, and that means I've had to make peace with the mullet, Australia's national hair trophy.

It seems like a rite of passage here, like thongs and meat pies. Every lad at some point decides it's time to try the "business up front, party in the back" approach, and honestly, I secretly love it. It's just another cousin of the Mohican to me, and there's a certain gleeful rebellion in those cascading tails. It's a haircut that says,

> "I take life seriously, but only as far back as the ears"

These days I've found myself in a bit of a niche market. With everyone going for longer locks, there was a shortfall of new stylists who could handle a proper short haircut. It's all surf-ready waves and Pinterest-inspired lengths, leaving today's young stylists with a void in their training. With fewer clients asking for bold, funky cuts, there's not enough practice for the up-and-comers to feel confident when someone asks for something with some edge. So, I'm the one who gets the call when someone wants a classic crop or a proper quiff - basically, anything shorter than shoulder length that requires a bit of flair.

But, a special shout out to the younger stylists these days. They're all long hair specialists, blonding gurus, and balayage wizards, pick a title, and they've got it.

Let's be real: modern colouring isn't your grandma's rinse-and-go. Today's transformations are pure art, complete with premium products that cost as much as a nice bottle of champagne. You'll find these stylists tethered to a single head of hair for three to seven hours, slinging foils, mixing toners, and tapping roots. It's a marathon, not a sprint, but the result? Worth every minute.

Now, prices have shot up because these treatments are multi-step masterpieces. With the applications, processing, and extra glossing touches, prices have doubled- and rightly so. So, ladies, if you're after these deluxe packages, just do the maths and respect the craft. It's not just a job; it's a wearable art.

And Me?

> I'm your go-to for curly girl and pixie cuts

– a speciality which keeps me on my toes. Don't get me wrong, I adore long hair work too, but I'm more than happy to share the workload with my crew of global cutting geniuses.

The best part? I know I'll be doing this as long as my hands will let me. Forty years in, and the thrill hasn't faded one bit.

People often ask, "Don't your feet get tired, standing all day?" Tired? My feet laugh in the face of tiredness. The thing that's kept me going all these years isn't willpower or sensible shoes – it's my devotion to netball for the last thirty years.

I started in England and continue to play here in Australia, hopping between teams and leagues wherever I can. Playing in Oz added a fun twist. Blokes play too! I love the competition in divisions one and two, especially the mixed teams. There's nothing more satisfying than dodging a guy twice your size and outsmarting him with a cheeky intercept.

People sometimes don't get it: hairdressing all day, then diving into a match? Easy, I guess it's my religion and I've been training for it my whole life. I finish my shift, lace up, and can still outrun a teenager on Red Bull. Hairdressing and netball are the perfect match – precision, endurance and a few sprints. It's my spa break where my mind unwinds and resets for the next day.

30

DON'T YOU FORGET ABOUT ME
SIMPLE MINDS

EVEN THOUGH MATTY and Bernie have long since taken their final bows, their legacy is still vibrant in the memories of people who knew them well. They both passed many moons ago, strong in character, but ultimately weak in heart. Only in the physical sense, mind you, not spiritually.

Dad died first. The priest didn't even realise Mum and Dad were a married couple as they sat on opposite sides of the church.

All the same, Mum sent him off in true Irish style: plenty of pomp, whiskey, and just enough eye-rolling to make sure he got the message wherever he was. I shudder to think how Matty would've coped if the redhead had left this world before him. Bottom line, he had spent a lifetime struggling to get her attention, but somehow managed to create a further divide.

They both had that enduring devotion to family that kept them more or less under the same roof, without ever sugar-coating the state of affairs. Mum's honest, no-nonsense approach made them into comedy gold – a bizarre duet that people couldn't quite get enough of.

The dysfunction brought its strange charm; the hilarity kept people mesmerised.

Dad was working away half the time, and when he did make it home, he would promptly head out for a three-day bender. Prior to August 1988, pubs in the UK were generally not allowed to open throughout the hours of 3 pm - 5:30 pm. The young guys in town, though, held him in legendary regard, not just for his knack of finding places to drink during split pub hours, but for his endurance.

They pandered like idolaters, each one hoping to make it onto Matty's moonshine initiation list. It was an ultimate rite of passage. An event where you got invited back to our place to listen to Irish music and partake in a few rounds of potcheen chasers until your legs gave out and memories dissolved.

If you survived the night, you'd crawl out the door by 2 am. But the bragging rights the next day were pure gold. Down the pub, you'd lean in and say,

> "Guess what, lads, Matty killed me over the weekend. He spiked me good and proper."

And the lads would raise their pints in solemn respect, knowing you'd joined the exclusive hazy ranks of those who'd danced on the edge with the great Matty himself.

Dad's popularity was such that he managed to "turn" a local man Irish. Well, half-Irish, at least. Whenever Dad returned from one of his trips, this bloke's Yorkshire accent would morph into an Irish lilt.

It wasn't a full transformation. You'd get this strange hybrid of Yorkshire-Irish that left folks looking at him sideways. He was like the town's very own leprechaun in training, rolling his R's and dropping casual *top o' the mornings* in every conversation.

But a few whiskeys in, and he'd be spilling his heart to the pub about how he and my dad were,

> "Raised together in the bog!"

Arm slung around Dad's shoulder for effect. Now my father found the whole thing a bit uncomfortable, but couldn't help being entertained – especially as he knew he didn't have a thirteenth sibling.

The looks on people's faces when the dodgy 'Irish" accent made its appearance – priceless. It was like they were watching a foreign film with bad dubbing. But Barnsley folks? They've got a high tolerance for eccentricity and quirkiness. This half-baked Irish accent from a fully baked Yorkshireman? Just another charming character trait. He sparked some fun banter among the locals.

People would whisper, "Oh, I knew him before he went Irish." Of course, when Dad's *actual* Irish pals rolled in, things took a proper turn.

The Irish wore suits and ties, the full shebang. More than once, Dad would be out in the street "singing" (if you could call it that) Giving it full volume, arms in the air like he's leading a march and a bit worse for wear. Inevitably, this would land him in a night in the local police station for a "cooling off."

The officers were always considerate with their late-night call, assuming Mum would be distraught. Possibly pacing the house with worry. They'd gently break the news that her husband was "in their care."

Mum, not missing a beat, would respond,

> "Keep him, I've got four daughters here and we'd all rather have a bit of peace and quiet. Let him thaw out there "til morning."

And that was that. No tears, no pleas for mercy. If anything, she welcomed the night off. It wasn't her job to save him from himself.

And like I said, this wasn't the first time.

Matty was the kind of bloke who could turn a church service into a brawl and a quiet cuppa into a national emergency. So, it shouldn't have been surprising when he managed to get himself arrested at my mum's brother's funeral. Yes, you read that right: arrested at a funeral. Well actually, the after-hours after the crowds had dispersed, at least.

The wake was held at the town Catholic club, which, in a grand stroke of irony, shared a car park with the local police station. This meant that the official vehicles were crammed together with visiting mourners.

Enter my dad's best mate, an Irishman who, after respectfully raising a few glasses (or six) to toast the dearly departed, found his legs rebelling against himself in the car park. Down he went, flat out, just as the police decided to have a mosey over. And that's where it all started to go pear-shaped.

Now Dad, ever the loyal protector, saw two uniformed officers approaching his mate on the ground and assumed the worst. He was convinced they were about to haul his friend off for the heinous crime of having a few too many. So, with the spirit of dignity and decorum fitting for a funeral, he swung. And swung again, hurling himself at law enforcement. The officers had simply come to help a wobbly Irishman up off the ground and were confronting two men, neither making a lick of sense.

The result is Matty in cuffs, being frog-marched off to the police station.

Of course, the cherry on top was when a family friend working at the club got through to my mum on the phone, explaining the whole mess. In usual Bernadette style, the ever-supportive wife replied,

> "Go over there and tell them to keep him."

Just like that. As if returning a faulty appliance to the shop. But back to Bernadette's current plight.

The next morning he breezed through the door, fresh from The Clink, like a man on a mission. He quickly took a sobering hot shower before grabbing a quick fry-up to start his day, eager to make it to mass on time.

Irony at its best.

The kitchen was the battleground of the house, mainly because it was the one place Mum and Dad managed to cross paths at the same time, both dead set on cooking, and where they communicated through the dog as a negotiator. Normally, Mum – Bernadette – kept it classy, but this particular morning, Dad was in full-blown search and destroy mode, tearing through the cupboards, in a muttering temper, "Where's the frying pan?"... as if the dog was going to respond. Then, raising his tone further,

"Where's the bloody frying pan?"

Mum, without missing a beat, calls back,

> "It's up my arse! Can't you see the handle sticking out?"

I nearly choked.

Dad had this strange ability to bring out responses from Mum that you'd never hear in polite company.

She was usually so restrained, but he was her one exception.

Then there was the time my friend Jayne stayed over. I walked into the kitchen just as she was polishing off her full English. Dad had whipped up eggs, bacon, toast, tea, and the works. As she's getting up to leave, Dad, thumbing through his paper with a glance, asks,

"Where are you off to today?"

Jayne's threw me a sideways glance.

"I'm going home," she said. Dad squinted, giving her a double take. I step in, realising his mistake.

> "Dad, this is Jayne, not one of your daughters. She's my friend."

They stared at each other, unblinking. I know it was early, but he studied her like she'd switched identities right in front of him.

As she walked down the drive, fueled by her hearty English breakfast, she doubled over laughing, happy he would chat with her for thirty minutes if he thought she was one of his tribe.

FAST FORWARD A FEW MONTHS.

Holidays are always a chance to escape the grind, and mine felt like a mini travel documentary. Planes, trains, and automobiles—I ticked every box, short of hitching a ride on a donkey. Three weeks of gallivanting around with my old school buddy Helen in Greece had been a full-on adventure which left me sunburnt, and bursting with stories to tell.

The longest I had ever been absent.

So there I was, finally dragging myself home, rucksack in tow. I stepped through the door in my jean shorts and flip flops, peeling off my travel-weary grin, only to have my own father stare at me like I was a door-to-door salesman.

I walked in, expecting, you know, a, *"Hello, glad you're home!"* from my father.

Instead, he glanced up and inquired,

'What time did you go out today?"

I was like,

> "Dad, I've not been here for the best part of a month."

"Of course you have! Don't be daft now," he said, eyeing me suspiciously.

"I've been in the Greek Islands for three weeks."

Apparently, in his mind, I'd only popped out for milk. Never mind the tan lines, the backpack, or the distinct smell of bad decisions and airport duty-free. Nope. He was convinced he'd seen me just the other day, strolling through the living room like a ghost on a casual haunting. Bewildered doesn't quite cut it—flabbergasted, perhaps? Or just outright insulted that my three-week odyssey had made such a fleeting impression.

What's the point of coming back if no one even noticed you left? Next time, I'll just send a postcard to myself. "Greetings from wherever you think I am."

This was typical of the number of scenarios that played out in our house. I'd pull Mum in for a quick reality check to confirm what was real and what was Dad's ... creative memory. And this is the same man who bought me my first watch and taught me to tell the time, yet he barely seemed to know what decade he was in half the time.

Bernadette was the kind of solid character you could count on, like an oak tree, a tough exterior with a touch of soft marshmallow in the middle. She'd show up no matter what. But like everyone, she had her quirks.

Take one morning after a twelve-hour night shift. She'd come home, eaten her "supper" — a full-on cooked breakfast — and was nursing a cup of tea, eyeing her shoes as though they'd told her a secret.

Finally, she said,

"I was admiring my shoes at work when I noticed ... they're the same style with the same stitch pattern down the side. Only one's navy blue and the other one is black."

A closer look revealed another peculiarity: a slight height difference between the two heels. How did she pull that off, I thought, given that the slip-on court shoe with a wedge heel is supposed to be a "sensible" choice.

I said,

"Mum, never mind the colours, how do you feel about the height difference?"

I tried them on, putting on a little show, bobbing and

weaving about in her mismatched shoes. But Bernadette just laughed it off.

> "I must have been slightly off-kilter, I bet the patients probably thought I'd had a few gins before clocking in."

Still, it didn't slow her down. Snowstorms? Five-mile walks to work? *Pfft*. This woman would lace up her boots and march into work unfazed. The rest of us thought "walking five miles" was something you did for charity, not just to clock in. But Bernadette didn't think twice. Meanwhile, folks with cars were calling in saying they couldn't make it.

Her loyalty was paid off in the form of an NHS plaque for ten years without a sick day – not one sniffle. Four kids at home, a job that kept her on her feet, and she just tossed that plaque into a drawer, like it was a participation ribbon.

Even after retirement age, they encouraged her to stay on. And so she kept going in, making sure every lady got a red rose on her birthday. I once asked her why she bothered going in on those miserable blizzardy nights.

"Who's gonna look after them if I don't?"

Spoken like it was the most obvious thing in the world. Mum was full of those pearls of wisdom.

> "If someone gets in your way, go around them."

Followed by ...

"And if they're no good, keep away."

Another favourite was, "A pound of your own is worth ten of anyone else's." She was all about independence, and her lessons stuck with me. And, above all, "Always try to do the right thing."

My mum's standard parting mantra:

> "Watch your step, keep away from trouble."

It wasn't just a casual reminder—it was practically law. And then, just as I reached for the door, she'd add her signature move: "Put one there." She'd tap the side of her cheek, waiting expectantly for the ritual kiss—a silent contract that no matter where I went or what kind of mischief I found myself in, I'd still come back in one piece.

Even now, when I head off somewhere, I catch myself half-expecting to hear her voice, feel her tap on the cheek. Funny how something so small can anchor you so completely.

> So now I tell my clients, "If I don't turn up, assume I'm in a coffin somewhere …."

As far as I know, hairdressers aren't allowed to retire … Because if Bernadette can do it, I've got no excuse.

31

GYPSY

STEVIE NICKS

LOOKING BACK on my forty years in hairdressing, I can honestly say it's been a journey that has shaped me in many ways. Sometimes smooth, sometimes like an off-road adventure, where the wheels occasionally come off. I've been salon-based, gone mobile and now I've come full circle, working from home in Brisbane. Thanks, Renee!

In all that time, I've met nearly every type of person out there, and here's what I've learned.

People are only human, and humans are endlessly fascinating- especially when you've got scissors in one hand and their deepest secrets in your ear. Everyone has a story to tell, and my clients always go for the *'with therapy option'*. A good chat always passes the time, and I love hearing stories, from the good, the bad and the downright ugly. Honestly, between untangling hair matted by anxiety, and shaving heads for charity and the occasional mental breakdown (theirs, not mine, though it's been close), I've seen it all.

I've cut necklaces off necks and lost more earrings down the sink than I care to admit. I'm on a first-name basis with local plumbers. I've snipped the necks and the ears of kids who can't sit still. I've managed to bleach and dye clients' clothes despite the protective gowns (Pro tip: Don't wear your Sunday best to a hair appointment unless you want it tie-dyed.) And definitely not a polo neck top, that has to be pegged down like a tent to access your hairline.

Rocking up in a gym kit? No jewellery? Perfect!

Now, I pride myself on professionalism, but I'd be lying if I said I haven't turned up to work hungover. Scratch that, I've turned up once while still drunk. (Sorry to that client and eternal gratitude to my junior who carried me through that shift).

> And talk about tripping over my words and putting my foot in it. I never assume someone's age. Never.

Take it from me, the time I tried to give a lovely salon lady a pensioner discount, turns out – she was only fifty-one. Her face was a mixture of horror and confusion. I wanted to crawl and hide.

Another classic mix-up, "Mary, your son's here to pick you up!" I chirped one day. She, baffled, responded, "That's my husband Liz."

I won't lie, I died a little inside. He was mortified, she was mortified, and I was laughing nervously while wondering how much it would cost to change my name and flee the country.

One of my all-time favourite (and utterly mortifying) hair mishaps involved a bride.

Picture this: it was the end of her bridal practice appointment, where I had designed bespoke hair pieces to achieve the bridal look. Everything had gone swimmingly, and just as I was about to pat myself on the back, she pulled out a wig. She casually plopped it on her head and asked me to cut a quick fringe in it. No problem, I thought! Easy! Big mistake! Fast-forward to the next morning and I'm greeted by a selfie ... no, worse – a sad ominous selfie. Something was amiss, I could feel my stylist senses tingling.

It took me a full cup of coffee and some squinting to realise I'd accidently given her real hair a bonus fringe, and quite wonky ...and we absolutely did not need that fringe for the wedding, which was only three weeks away.

It was one of those ultra-glamorous top-tier weddings where the dress cost more than my first car, and now I was in full panic mode trying to figure out how I was going to undo my handiwork. On the wedding day, I took a few deep breaths. After some strategic twisting and pinning along with the kind of know-how that can only be learned at *Lizzi Mac's School of Hairdressing Wizardry*, I concealed the surplus strands. Susy and I now lovingly refer to it as "Fringe Gate".

These days Susy is a successful and wildly creative wedding planner based in Yorkshire, running her own empire "Sweet Spaces". She's the kind of woman who can take your budget and turn it into a wedding so stunning, it makes the Kardashians look like they planned theirs at a petrol station.

I imagine when she's sitting down with couples, discussing the endless ways their Big Day could go belly-up, *Fringe Gate* gets a special mention.

After all, nothing says "professional crisis handler," quite like someone who's lived through a full-blown bridal meltdown over unwanted wonky bangs.

After navigating that disaster, she's prepared for any number of catastrophes – flaming cakes, feuding families, or a missing groom. And though it's all bespoke venues, fairy-lit lanterns, and artisanal cupcakes, I like to think that every centrepiece and twinkly aisle is just a hint of the scrappy and unique, can-do brilliance that's always made Susy.... Well, Susy.

Much of my career has been mobile hairdressing, which sounds glamorous until you realise it involves lugging your kit in and out of people's houses while trying not to trip over their Labradoodle. But it's given me the unique experience of weaving myself into the very fabric of people's lives.

You see, mobile hairdressers don't just do hair – we get involved. I love that mobile work has given me the freedom to be at the school gates for my girls. I've had the lucky fortune of attending every event in their school lives and being there to greet them at the end of each day. It's a bloody juggling act though. I was back to work eight weeks after giving birth – twice.

How, you ask? Simple: electric breast pump in the car boot, cool box and ice blocks at the ready, and the attitude of a woman who'd fight a bear for five minutes of sleep. Yes, ladies, you can have the versatility of structuring your work calendar and dual-feed your babies. Pump milk whilst your foils are processing, whilst your little one is being topped up on a bottle somewhere else in your absence. Just don't forget your bottle of wine on a Friday night when you dump that milk down the sink – back to business on Monday like nothing ever happened.

Then there's the clients' husbands and their fascination with the engineering marvel that is the electric breast pump.

It's like the Discovery Channel suddenly lost its appeal. "Wow, how does that work?" And there's always one joker, "What's it like in coffee?" (Top tip: don't try it.)

Being a mobile hairdresser means venturing into people's homes, and trust me, no two homes are the same. You get an up close and personal look at the inner workings of their family politics – something salon stylists rarely get to see.

Every six weeks, I walk in, put the kettle on, and they don't even pause. Not even when a family argument is in full swing. "It's only Lizzi." I'm like an invisible referee in the background. In fact – I've often been roped into solving the odd family crisis.

"Lizzi, can you talk to my teenager? They will listen to you."

Because if I can cut hair, I'm also qualified to do teenage exorcisms. I've been there for break-ups and make-ups. I once arrived at a mobile colour appointment for a regular client to find her husband simply rocking in a chair

"She's not here," he mumbled. "She's run off with her fancy man!"

Naturally, I had to take a seat and play therapist for thirty minutes.

"Don't worry mate, she'll be back."

It's all part of the service, right?

Then there are the more unusual requests, like when someone tosses me a waxing kit and says,

> "C'mon Liz, it's Brazilian o'clock! I need this lot off. I'm going on holiday and on the last push. How are you fixed?"

32

THAT'S WHAT FRIEND'S ARE FOR
DIONNE WARWICK

HOW AM I FIXED?

Well, mentally unprepared. But when someone's half-naked and kicking their underwear off, I sigh, grab the wax strips and get on with it.

I do consider myself lucky to have reigned in this creative space for as long as I have. It's a job for the motivated, the organised, and the slightly unhinged.

You're revamping and transforming people daily, and let's be honest, everyone loves a relaxing head massage. I've mastered the art of making it look effortless while internally planning my next holiday.

My heartfelt thanks go out to all of you who've sat in my chair, and more impressively, kept coming back. You've trusted me to be your stylist, your therapist, your friend, and, on some occasions, your secret keeper. And the sweet spot is we can't ever fall out, as we know too much about each other. It's a true noble gift I've always treasured.

My other very special takeaway – to all the stylists I've met along the way — I hope we've shared more than just a salon floor. Whether it was a clever trick with scissors, a life lesson over lukewarm coffee, or a much-needed laugh when the chips were down. I'd like to think we left each other better than we found each other. We've had each other's backs through botched colour corrections, messy love lives, family dramas, shift-swapping marathons, and everything in between. Let's face it - we're more than stylists. We're the ultimate crew, the dream team. And we bloody know it.

Amongst all this experience, I have collected a few messages, some food for thought and hopefully a little bit of wisdom. I often wonder what hairdressing will look like in fifty years' time. Will we be using telepathic scissors that can style your hair with just a thought? Maybe clients will want hair that changes colour based on their mood, or even the strength of your Wi-Fi connection. So, neon pink because their signal is strong, next they're a sombre grey and buffering as they walk.

Too busy for a real appointment? Not a problem. Clients will send a hologram of their heads requesting some "cosmic waves please".

And how about mixing science with science? DNA based hair – spit into a tube, and seconds later, their "perfect" hairstyle will be revealed, along with some uncomfortable truths.

> "You have the hair genes for mullets... and a slight tendency towards Lemmy-style mutton chops. I'm so sorry."

Personally, wouldn't it be brilliant if — and this is for hairdressers and barbers only — we could take our heads off and style ourselves? As we get tired of chopping and slapping our own colour on. I mean, really, we spend all day making other people look fabulous, but when it comes to our turn, we're knackered. Pop the head off, give it a trim, slap it back on, and job done. Sounds like the next logical step.

The futuristic vision may surprise us, but one thing will never change: clients will still be late for appointments, and hairdressers will still have to deal with,

> "I want a drastic change, but don't want to lose any length or layers and I want to stay the same colour."

I usually suggest they go home, rearrange their furniture and redecorate their lounge, if they fancy a "drastic change." At least the cushions won't argue back.

So, when you think of your hairdresser, don't just picture us snipping away and making small talk. Picture us as artists, scientists, and maybe even a little bit like wizards, using our special code to transform the ordinary into the extraordinary.

We are alchemists.

COULDN'T FINISH this chapter without reflecting on me and Ann—lifelong friends, and what a pair! Even though I'm soaking up the Aussie sun and she's across the pond in the States, we're still Sissys to the core, bonded by a lifetime of glorious chaos and shared mischief. Our friendship?

Think Absolutely Fabulous—equal parts wild humour and bulletproof loyalty. We don't just laugh at Edina and Patsy; we are Edina and Patsy, ticking off their antics like a highlight reel of our own escapades.

We've seen it all—scaled the heights, crawled through the lows, and somehow managed to come out the other side with our sense of humour gloriously intact. The best part? We can bring each other to the brink of hysterics with just a single word.

One word is all it takes to set off the kind of laughter that leaves us gasping for air, tears streaming, and thoroughly convinced that the other is a genius. Everyone else? They stare, bewildered, like we've lost the plot (we have). But you can tell - they'd sell their left arm to be in on it.

We've always been each other's sounding board—the go-to for relationship dramas and every sticky situation life throws our way. You could rip out our fingernails and toenails one by one, and we still wouldn't turn on each other. Loyalty like ours doesn't budge.

Men come and go, chaos ebbs and flows, but through it all, we're always ready—locked and loaded, getaway car idling, and a shovel in the boot, just in case. Some friendships are casual. Ours? Ride or die. Literally.

Not a day passes without some perfectly-timed meme or heartfelt message from Ann lighting up my inbox. It's her way of reminding me that the little Mikes of life truly don't matter. And she's right—she always is. That's Ann for you.

To the nursing home that lands us, let me say: brace yourselves. Hand us a guitar, and we'll be *Kum ba Yah-ing* like pros. (Never mind that neither of us knows a single chord; we'll find a way to make beautiful noise together.)

> Just slide a tray of good wine and food outside the door and consider yourselves lucky. It's going to be fabulous.

33

HERO

MARIAH CAREY

BING BONG!

Attention passengers on flight 10/81. This is Captain Lizzi Mac speaking. As we make our final descent, I'd like to share a few thoughts from my 40-year journey with you. Please remove the information leaflet from the seat in front of you, and turn the page to see my top tips for my fellow hair crew.

LIZZI MAC'S TOP TIPS FOR MY FELLOW HAIR CREW

1. REMEMBER YOU WORK IN A TEAM. Even if you are a solo artist, your family is your team.
2. ALWAYS DO YOUR BEST WORK. Even if you're running a bit late.
3. LOOK AFTER YOUR SENIOR STYLISTS, and they will nurture you.
4. LOOK AFTER YOUR JUNIORS. You are their mentor.
5. KEEP YOU SCISSORS SHARP, and your service even sharper.
6. ALWAYS KEEP A STASH OF BAND AIDS. You'll be constantly nicking yourself with the scissors ... too late once there's a smear down the collar of your client's shirt or blouse. Nothing says *"relaxing salon experience"* quite like the stylist hovering over you muttering *"Don't worry, just checking for blood."*
7. DON'T THROW SICKIES. It's tempting but remember – karma has a pair of scissors too, so don't let the team down.
8. ALWAYS CARRY SNACKS. They're the lifeblood of every hairdresser. Carry a stash

or raid client's fridges. Keep those energy levels up!

9. **DON'T LEAVE HAIR CUTTINGS NEXT TO THE HAIR BIN.** It makes me wonder what state your bikini line is in. Let's keep things tidy, shall we?

10. **DON'T LET HAIR BUILD UP ON YOUR TROLLEY WHEELS.** It's a slow-growing fungus and makes me wonder what your bikini line is like and your armpits.

11. **PUT EVERYTHING BACK IN EXACTLY THE SAME PLACE.** There's a special place in hell for the ones who don't, along with the ones who steal sectioning clips.

12. **BE CLIENT FOCUSED.** They are paying your wages, and yes, sometimes it feels like you've earned every single penny, but they'll tip better if you actually care.

13. **WHEN YOU GO ON HOLIDAY.** Don't let anyone rope you into a daily itinerary- you've spent the entire year running on other people's schedules, this is your time to be free.

14. **AND ABOVE ALL, BE HAPPY.** You're changing so many lives, one head at a time,

and that's no small feat. Whether it's giving someone the confidence to go on that first date or helping them feel a little more human after a rough time, you're leaving your mark on their spirits – and their roots.

SO, there you have it – forty years of hairdressing wisdom distilled. What's kept me going all this time?

Well, it's a tapestry of moments – the odd, the uplifting, and the downright exhausting. The people too of course, including the ones that never paused for breath, which is why I have developed impressive lip-reading skills, even if they're chewing gum. Of course, there's the hair itself. The endless parade of textures, colours, and shapes, each as unique as the head it's attached to.

> But here's the thing I've come to believe: we manifest what we want and what we need, even if we don't realise it at the time.

What you feel in your heart and your path to success are like a pair of scissors in perfect sync – inseparable.

> Trust your journey, mould your future, and work with the universe rather than against it. Every experience, even the tough ones, has something to teach, some bit of wisdom tucked away for the taking. You can't dodge life's rough edges – you grow by facing them.

And now, here I am in Queensland, living the dream in the land of eternal sunshine. Still behind the chair; and still in the game.

And remember, if everything else fails, just put on some 80's music.

Touchdown, folks. Thanks for flying with us on flight 10/81. We hope you've enjoyed your time with us, and look forward to seeing you again in the future. This has been your captain, Lizzi Mac speaking.

Safe travels!

ACKNOWLEDGMENTS

To my parents, who taught me resilience, humour, and the value of hard work – thank you for the roots that kept me grounded and the wings to help me chase my dreams. Your love and unwavering belief in me shaped everything I am and strive to be. You are and always will be, the heart of my story.

To my sister Angela – whose name fittingly carries the word 'Angel' – you are my rock, my confidante, and my greatest cheerleader. You are the sister everyone dreams of, and I'm beyond lucky to call you mine.

And my two beautiful daughters, the radiant stars of my life, who inspire me every day with their brilliance, warmth, and uniquely wonderful selves:

My Eldest – My Baby (Yes, you'll always be the baby, no matter what!). A guiding star and an unstoppable force of nature. Your courage and strength are awe-inspiring.

My youngest—my Dolly, the 'lady in waiting' and cherished baby friend to her big sister. Your boundless strength, spark, and razor-sharp wit bring endless joy, making our world infinitely brighter.

I may be your teacher, but you've both been incredible teachers to me –showing me love without limits, strength in vulnerability, loyalty beyond compare, and finding beauty in the smallest moments.

Stay as you are,
fearless, funny, and fabulous.

This book is for my family,
who made me, shaped me,
and continue to make me proud.

DEAR READER
A LITTLE FAVOUR IF YOU DON'T MIND.

Writing this book has been a labour of love, and I truly hope it's brought a smile to your face, or at least made you smirk awkwardly in public.

If you enjoyed it, could I cheekily ask you to leave me a positive review? Just a few words about what you liked would mean the world. Think of it as a virtual high-five and a wink to the girl behind the chair.

And if you think your friends might enjoy it, give them a nudge too. Thanks for sticking with me — you're officially part of the Hair Crew.

Cheers,

Lizzi Mac

Linktree to stay in touch

www.ingramcontent.com/pod-product-compliance
Lightning Source LLC
Chambersburg PA
CBHW060549080526
44585CB00013B/498